You Are the Brand

Endorsements

"Smart, practical, and a bold call to authenticity and integrity in the world of personal branding. *You Are the Brand* brings razor-sharp clarity to the often vague and mysterious expert industry like no other book out there. This isn't just a practical how-to book; it's a behind-the-scenes look at the industry and is a needed challenge to higher integrity and authenticity in a world of image and social media followers."

Pat Flynn
Founder, SmartPassiveIncome.com

"Mike Kim unpacks the most basic truth about branding for entrepreneurs: You are the brand. In the pages of this book, you'll discover how to create a unique public identity that will build your platform and strengthen your offer. And if you think there's nothing brand-worthy about you, think again. *You Are the Brand* will walk you through the process of creating a compelling personal brand to build your business around."

Michael Hyatt
New York Times bestselling author *Platform* and *The Vision Driven Leader*

"Mike Kim does more in *You Are the Brand* than help us brand ourselves; he helps us figure out how we can be useful in the world. And being useful leads to a sense of purpose and meaning."

Donald Miller
New York Times bestselling author
CEO, StoryBrand

"Mike Kim is proof that it is possible to do what I've been saying for years: to reinvent yourself and build a career that showcases your unique expertise, passion, and experience. *You Are the Brand* is packed with actionable, proven steps to help you do exactly that!"

Dorie Clark
Bestselling author of *Reinventing You*
Faculty, Duke University Fuqua School of Business

"If you have been looking for a field guide on how to build a brand and business that will not only grow but stand the test of time, then *You Are the Brand* is your new business and marketing bible."

Dana Malstaff
Founder, Boss Mom

"Mike Kim has done it again! He now has turned his genius toward teaching how any person with a message can build their personal brand. Having worked with Mike and benefited from his 'out of the box' thinking, which has generated millions of dollars, I can say that *You Are the Brand* will be the most productive book you will read this year and beyond."

Paul Martinelli
CEO, Empowered Living
Cofounder, The John Maxwell Team

"Here is a book that challenges our assumptions about what a personal brand is, how this weird world of marketing really works, and why the best strategy for success is telling the truth. Bravo. We have needed this book for a very long time, and I'm so glad it's finally here."

Jeff Goins
Bestselling author of *Real Artists Don't Starve*

"If you've ever watched a professional speaker on stage and wondered how they made the jump from amateur to expert, this book is for you. Full of inspiring and motivating stories, *You Are the Brand* is for anyone hoping to take a risk and see where monetizing their expertise can take them."

Laurie Ruettimann
Bestselling author of *Betting On You*

"Mike has an otherworldly way of breaking down branding and business in a simple and actionable way. If you've ever struggled to figure out how to build a brand that stands out in a competitive market and feels like the best version of you, Mike's got you covered with *You Are the Brand*."

Kira Hug
Cofounder, The Copywriter Club

"In *You Are the Brand*, Mike Kim gives away all of his secrets. Reading You Are the Brand is like sitting with him over dinner and having him thoroughly explain every important strategy and tactic you need to create a personal brand—one that is heartfelt, unique, and attractive to the people you most want to help."

Ernie Svenson, Esq.
Founder, Law Firm Autopilot

"If you are ready to invest in yourself and build a business that will pay dividends for the rest of your life, then *You Are the Brand* is for you. Mike Kim is my go-to expert on all things personal branding, so get ready for your brand to never be the same!"

Jamal Miller
CEO, Miller Media Group

"Mike Kim is a clear and proven expert who helps people market and monetize their personal experience, ideas, and wisdom. Finally, he has condensed his know-how and experience into this 'must read' book, *You Are the Brand.*"

Ray Edwards
Bestselling author of *How to Write Copy That Sells*

"*You Are the Brand* is a riveting example of Mike Kim's marketing brilliance in a consumable and implementable format. This is a must-read for all experts, coaches, and consultants who want to elevate their brand and generate new clients. You Are the Brand is a no-nonsense guide to marketing your company's most valuable asset, YOU."

Dr. Krista Burns
Founder, The American Posture Institute
TEDx speaker

"It's not often you come across a book that leaves you this informed and inspired. The next time I'm asked for advice on how to build a brand as an expert, the next eight words out of my mouth will be, 'Read *You Are the Brand* by Mike Kim.'"

Dr. Carrie Rose
Cofounder, of-course.us

"Whether you're looking to become a sought-after consultant, get up on stage, or influence people to live a better life, *You Are the Brand* is the guidebook you've been looking for."

Rich Brooks
Founder, Agents of Change Digital Marketing Conference
President, Flyte New Media

"*You Are the Brand* lays out the exact steps you need to showcase your unique expertise, and it's written by someone who actually lives and breathes these steps. Mike Kim has taken his genius and put his 'school of hard knocks' experience into this book so that any of us can apply these same principles to grow and thrive."

Dr. Mark T. Wade
Founder, Virtual Summits Software

"Reading *You Are the Brand* by Mike Kim is like taking a deep breath of reality. The content is fresh, exciting, and empowers you to build your personal brand. As someone who works with many small businesses and personal brands, I can say without a doubt that this is the 'no B.S.' book we have been waiting for."

Lauren V. Davis
CEO, Lauren Davis Creative
Cofounder, #SocialROCKConf

"*You Are the Brand* is long overdue! I've used Mike's strategies to help countless nonprofit leaders and their organizations connect with their donors using stories that convey authenticity, warmth, and clarity. This book couldn't have come at a better time."

Mary Valloni
Cofounder, Fully Funded Academy

"Every speaker, coach, consultant, or trainer should do more than read *You Are the Brand*––they should study it. This is THE system for building a profitable personal brand business. The bonus? Mike's style is practical, simple, and funny."

Daniela Nica
Founder, The MentorMind Community

"We can see it now: a highlighted, Post-It laden, dog-eared copy of *You Are the Brand* in the hands of every budding entrepreneur seeking to build a personal brand. Mike Kim has written a brilliant, simple to understand, and easy to implement guidebook for creating lasting success. Get your copy and start highlighting!"

Kay Salerno & Shila Morris
Sister Entrepreneurs Co-owners, Squeeze In Restaurant Group

"Mike's proven framework is forged from experience and expertise in the field with real people and real businesses. *You Are the Brand* is a guidebook that offers hope without hype. Shave decades off your branding journey by reading and applying this masterpiece."

Kary Oberbrunner
Bestselling author of *Elixir Project* and *Unhackable*

YOU ARE THE BRAND

The 8-Step Blueprint to Showcase Your
Unique Expertise and Build a Highly
Profitable, Personally Fulfilling Business

Mike Kim

NEW YORK

LONDON • NASHVILLE • MELBOURNE • VANCOUVER

You Are the Brand

The 8-Step Blueprint to Showcase Your Unique Expertise and Build a Highly Profitable, Personally Fulfilling Business

Published in New York, New York, by Morgan James Publishing. Morgan James is a trademark of Morgan James, LLC. www.MorganJamesPublishing.com

A **FREE** ebook edition is available for you or a friend with the purchase of this print book.

CLEARLY SIGN YOUR NAME ABOVE

Instructions to claim your free ebook edition:
1. Visit MorganJamesBOGO.com
2. Sign your name CLEARLY in the space above
3. Complete the form and submit a photo of this entire page
4. You or your friend can download the ebook to your preferred device

ISBN 9781631953477 paperback
ISBN 9781631953484 eBook
Library of Congress Control Number:
2020947371

Book Design by:
Jason Clement
jasonclement.com

with...
Habitat for Humanity®
Peninsula and Greater Williamsburg

Morgan James is a proud partner of Habitat for Humanity Peninsula and Greater Williamsburg. Partners in building since 2006.

Get involved today! Visit
MorganJamesPublishing.com/giving-back

*Haru and Taeho, you bring so much joy to my life
and remind me to live in the moment. Uncle Mike loves you.
I can't wait to take you monsters to Disney World one day.*

*Esther, I'm one lucky brother to have a sister like you.
Now that the book is done, we can drink wine all night again.*

*Mom, thanks for your unending love and support. I hope this book
makes you famous because I put a lot of stories in it about you.*

*Dad, thanks for instilling in me a love
for reading and writing since I was young.*

Contents

Foreword

I first came into contact with Mike Kim's "branding brain" at a conference in Puerto Rico. We were both speakers at an event, and as we stood by the pool talking, we started discussing the mistakes people make when building a brand for themselves in today's overly polished world.

For twenty-three years, I've been coaching and mentoring elite pro athletes, leaders, and public figures on the topics of performance, strategy, mindset, and execution.

I've had a front-row seat to see how the mistakes people make, some unknowingly, can end up costing them their careers or, equally as sad, can cause them to dislike the world they've created for themselves. (When you've spent more than two decades reshaping elite performers' identities, using scientific methods, and done 18,000+ hours of one-on-one coaching, the leap into personal branding isn't very far.)

I help someone tell a better story about who they are so they can perform at peak levels on Olympic stages, in the NBA finals, or in boardrooms. It isn't much different than the work Mike Kim does. He helps experts craft a better (and true) story through creating a personal brand.

As he rightly points out, *everyone already is a personal brand*. But how you choose to cultivate that brand is a choice: Ignore it and let the world decide who you are, or be intentional and bring your best self forward.

Imagine showing up in the world more excited about the work you do because you know it's more congruent with how you'd like to be known and who you are at your core.

It's freeing.

You don't need to cultivate some perfect persona of someone with zero faults or be someone who can solve every problem thrown your way. That stuff is from a playbook discarded years ago, after the vomit-inducing era of "influencers." While you may still hear the word *influencer* used, the playbook today is *very* different. Mike was the first person I heard codify it in a practical, useable, and results-focused way.

When we were standing by the pool, Mike shared the three basic questions he used to help major personal brands break through the marketing noise. He calls it the PB3, which you'll find in chapter three.

That's when I knew he was a legit expert.

Only someone with deep experience in the fires of real-world execution could distill such a simple concept down to something so immediately practical. It's the classic Einstein Effect: "If you can't explain it simply, you don't understand it well enough."

Since we met that day, Mike has revealed more of his frameworks, branding tools, and genius with me. I've invited Mike to speak at my conferences and events because the entrepreneurs who attend always leave with clarity, concepts, and a renewed conviction to take the right action for them. One of our attendees said it well: *"He's just so darn smart and helpful."*

If you use the frameworks, tools, and exercises Mike has laid out for you in this lean book, don't hate him because it seems so simple or he hasn't given you more work to do. That's what true experts do: identify the key components that help you achieve more with less.

Enjoy the opportunities, wins, and profits from *You Are the Brand*!

Todd Herman
Author, *Wall Street Journal* and International Best Seller,
The Alter Ego Effect: The Power of Secret Identities to Transform Your Life

My Story

A while back, I was talking with a friend and telling them I was writing a book on building a personal brand business—basically a book on showcasing your unique ideas, expertise, reputation, and personality, and then creating a business around that collective identity. My friend asked me a simple but provocative question: "What feeling do you want the reader to get when they read your book?"

My immediate response was: "*Finally!*"

By that I mean I want someone to get the sense they've finally found what's going to help them—step by step—get where they want to go without having to suffer through costly mistakes. I want them to have the feeling they've been unlocked, to feel excitement swell up from within, and to feel a sense of hope that the career and life they've dreamed of is within reach.

Because that wasn't always true for me.

In late 2012, I returned to Piscataway, New Jersey, after I resigned from a four-year music director job at a church in Hartford, Connecticut. Life had come full circle; I moved back into the same cramped condo where I had lived before, just minutes from where

I had graduated college. The only difference: I was four years older and four years more lost.

Enter my so-called life: Thirty-four years old, no job, no direction, draining my savings, drowning in an embarrassing amount of debt, and still trying to figure out: *"What am I going to do with my life?"*

So, I did what I usually do when I feel lost—I read *a lot* of books.

Books have changed my life. But when I was going through my own life transitions, particularly in my professional life, I couldn't find exactly what I needed to help me. I made countless trips to my local Barnes & Noble looking for books that talked about starting a completely new career in the "expert" space.

Looking for these books was like trying to push glue up a hill. I couldn't really find any that met me exactly where I was.

Sure, there were books on finding a new career like Richard Bolles' *What Color Is Your Parachute?* that sell year after year. But that wasn't quite it. I didn't want to find a new job; I wanted to create my own business, one that was a reflection of who I am and what I wanted out of life.

I found a handful of books that inspired me to keep pursuing my dreams, like Dorie Clark's excellent title *Reinventing You*. But what I really wanted were "how-to" books where I could learn exactly what to do and how to do it. Surely the people whose books lined the shelves at Barnes & Noble built an "expert" business for themselves!

My frustration mounted with every new book I bought. I hated it when books said, "Decide what problem you want to solve, and go find clients" without giving any concrete examples of how to do that. (Why couldn't they just say, "This is the exact email I would send if I were starting all over again"?)

I hated it when copywriters (people who write marketing materials and ads) would only teach broad principles or give fill-in-the-blank templates because, yet again, they didn't provide actual campaigns that I could take and tweak to apply to my own situation.

I especially hated it when the personal development books said, "Picture who you want to be in a few years!" but didn't provide a practical pathway to get clarity.

Much of my frustration was rooted in the simple fact that by that point in my life, I didn't need more convincing. I didn't need more inspiration. I just literally wanted to know what to do and what to say in a step-by-step manner. No wonder I've always loved those yellow "For Dummies" books. They had a way of explaining a topic in simple, logical ways!

What I was really looking for was a blueprint that would combine the personal development piece (who I am), the business development piece (what I have to offer), and the marketing piece (the art and skills to persuade someone to take action).

Now let me shift here for a moment and tell you about how I got to the point of wanting to start my own "expert" business.

After working a few jobs out of college, I had taken a position as the music director of the church near Hartford. My job was to lead the music portion of weekly services, recruit and rehearse volunteer musicians, and write songs that would have mass appeal to our congregation and other churches.

I wasn't aware of it at the time, but I was intuitively using marketing principles to do all of those things. Everything I did— from recruiting "free-spirited" musicians, writing simple music that would be accessible to the everyday person, spearheading numerous conferences, to promoting our music albums—all had to do with marketing.

Mind you, I wasn't a trained musician. Other than a few years of piano lessons as a child, I never really knew how music worked. I just had a knack for it. But when I took a music theory class in college, I was stunned.

I learned what a relative major is and what a relative minor is. I learned the different types of scales and time signatures. My head kind of exploded! I knew music as art, but I was amazed to learn the actual science and methodology behind creating music. Music is like math—it's replicable because there is form and structure to it. But music is also art—it touches the heart. It's a lot like marketing!

A few years later, I went through an unexpected career change, which I'll share a bit more in detail later. The short story is that I resigned from my music director position, moved back to New Jersey, and took a part-time teaching job at an after-school academy (the same place I used to work at in my early twenties) helping high school students prepare for their college entrance exams.

One day as I was walking out the door, something made my boss say, "Mike, do you have a moment to take a look at this ad for our academy?"

I told her, "Sure." Then I proceeded to say, "Actually, the design isn't good because it's not very clear what you guys are promoting here. This font needs to be bigger. The message is buried. But most of all, you haven't communicated what value someone is going to get if they enroll their child here."

She was astonished because she didn't realize I knew anything about this kind of stuff. The truth was, I didn't, not formally at least. But I had an instinct for it.

She paused for a moment and then asked me to sit down. Her words changed the course of my life. She said, "Mike, I want you to take over all of the marketing for the entire company. Name your price."

After a nanosecond of shock, I pulled a number out of the air (it was a lot) and said I wanted to be the Chief Marketing Officer. And I got the job.

Since I didn't have a formal marketing education, I devoured every marketing book I could, especially on copywriting. I read all the classic "Mad Men" era books by authors like John Caples, David Ogilvy, and Eugene Schwartz.

But the book that had the most impact was an old, classic marketing book, *Ogilvy on Advertising*.

It was through reading this book that I came to realize I had been doing marketing all my life. Apparently my "on the job" marketing training happened when I was hosting conferences, promoting albums, and persuading volunteers to join the music team back when I worked at the church.

The stuff I learned from these books and applied to the company's marketing helped us dramatically increase revenue within the first year, and it certainly helped me look really good at work!

But I still wanted more. I hadn't moved back to New Jersey just to trade one job for another. I wanted freedom. I wanted to create impact with my ideas. I wanted to do work that I loved and believed in. If I'm really honest, I never wanted to work in an office or commute to work ever again!

While those old "Mad Men" era books helped me learn marketing in a more formal manner, none of them were geared toward a "solopreneur" because the solopreneur didn't exist back then. But that's who I really wanted to be.

As I continued learning, I discovered more contemporary marketers (and solopreneurs) like Michael Hyatt, Ray Edwards, Amy Porterfield, and Pat Flynn, to name a few. I invested in learning from the best (and I'm now privileged to call some of them friends), but I also discovered there was something more to them than just their ideas.

Granted, they were all very different—Michael was a former corporate CEO, Ray was a former radio host, Amy worked for personal development guru Tony Robbins, and Pat was a former architect. But they all had something intangible that they were able to communicate to the marketplace.

What did they all have in common?

The answer is actually quite comforting. They were able to build their businesses around their ideas, expertise, reputation, and personalities. The blend of all these things made each of them unique and unable to be copied. What they had to offer was *unique to each of them.*

This idea was reinforced for me recently when I interviewed Rick Barker, one of pop star Taylor Swift's early managers. Before Taylor became a global icon, she was just a talented, normal person. When I asked Rick what made her stand out upon first meeting her, he said she had "something intangible."

The good news is we all have something intangible that makes us unique. Some of these things are physical. Some are intellectual. Some of these things have to do with our skills, demeanor, or personality. This is why we like some actors more than others, some basketball players more than others, and why some people prefer Taylor Swift over Katy Perry. It's more than just their music or about who the "best" actor, player, or singer in the world is— it's about who they are as people. It's about their brand.

For all this talk of branding, one important thing to consider is that actors, athletes, and pop megastars aren't paid directly by moviegoers or fans in the seats. They're paid by their production companies, record labels, or the team they play for.

On the other hand, you and I are going to be paid directly by the people we serve—our clients and customers. As a result, there are additional considerations to account for when we start to build a *business* around ourselves.

It's not going to be easy, but if you build your personal brand with intention, you truly can create a highly profitable and personally fulfilling business. You truly can change your life while changing other people's lives, and I truly believe this is one of the most noble ways to make a living.

That's why over the last number of years, I've focused on creating a personal brand for myself and others, and after much testing, tweaking, and refining, I'm writing the "how to" book I was searching for all those years ago.

But it's also important for me to tell you what this book is *not*: It's not a book about image.

Instead, You Are the Brand *is a book about building a business around your ideas, expertise, reputation, and personality—through building relationships.* I often say that marketing isn't about closing a sale, it's about opening a relationship. You open relationships with potential clients and partners by sharing yourself in an authentic way, not by hawking some doctored-up image of yourself.

What I'm offering here is a way to dig deep and identify *your own personal brand*: I'll help you discover who you are, what you have to offer, and how to market your ideas.

It's going to take work (and a bit of vulnerability) on your part. It's easy to think, "Great! Once I have this all figured out, I'll start." Nope. I'm going to ask you to start and figure it out as you go, with me alongside you as your guide. You may find yourself referring back to this book weeks, months, or even years from now—and I encourage you to do so.

There's a reason I refer to the method herein as a "blueprint." No builder looks at a blueprint just once and then builds the entire skyscraper. No, the blueprint is there to keep construction on track over the course of the entire project. My hope is that you will use this book in the same fashion.

Let's get to work, friend. Keep in mind that the more you put yourself out there, the more you will start to discover yourself. As you read *You Are the Brand*, it's my hope that you'll breathe a deep sigh and think to yourself, "Finally! This is what I've been looking for. I can do this!"

If you'd like to download a free companion guide to *You Are the Brand* complete with editable templates, swipe files, and examples, go to YouAreTheBrandBook.com.

PART ONE

The Personal Brand

CHAPTER ONE

Who Do You Have to Become in Order to Serve the People You Want to Serve?

I was in high school during the early days of the internet when web browsers like America Online (AOL) and Netscape were all the rage. I still remember interacting with strangers in chatrooms, reading blogs (Xanga, anyone?), and keeping up with friends through AOL Instant Messenger—or AIM, for short.

AIM was a chatting app that was a precursor to the direct messaging features found on most social media platforms today. One summer, all of my friends seemed to catch the AIM bug. Everyone I knew seemed to have an account, and the fear of missing out hit me big time. AIM was the place to be!

I scrounged through my family's mail to track down one of the free discs that America Online was sending out in those days. I grabbed our telephone cord, plugged it into the computer, and fired up that snail-paced modem ready to join the party that was apparently happening on Instant Messenger!

Suddenly I stopped completely in my tracks, my face frozen by what I saw on the screen.

I had to create a username for my AIM account.

Laugh if you will, but I'm positive I'm not the only person who was terrified at the prospect of having to create my own username.

I must have stared at the screen for at least half an hour trying to come up with something cool and witty. My username *had* to be cool because I had friends to impress, and if I'm really honest, I wanted girls to think, "Mike is so witty! He's so cute! I think I'll marry him!"

After what seemed like an eternity, I came up with the perfect username. It would be powerful! It would project manliness! It would sound unique! It would be a clever play on my first name, and girls would surely bombard me with requests for dates! My AIM username would be...

Mikovitch!

(Stop laughing.)

Things didn't work out the way I imagined. In fact, they completely backfired. All of my friends thought it was the dumbest username ever. One of my buddies asked if I was trying to sound like a Russian guy, and from that point on whenever I saw my so-called friends in person, they mocked me with a military salute shouting, "Greetings, Comrade Mikovitch!"

The final moment of humiliation was when a girl I really liked said she had an even better username for me: "Miko*bitch*." I still remember her chuckling at me. (Whatever, I'm a grown man now, and she's probably living a miserable exis-- oh, never mind.)

For as long as the internet has been around, people have been obsessed with how they present themselves online. We want to come across well. We want people to like us. We want, in marketing terms, to build a brand.

As you may know, "branding" stems from the old ranching practice of burning an identifying mark onto livestock with an iron. The concept of branding later expanded into business and marketing to identify products manufactured by a particular company under a particular name.

Josiah Wedgwood, an English potter born in the 1700s who is often called the father of modern marketing, was perhaps the first person who leveraged branding to create a retail empire. After winning a competition hosted by Queen Charlotte, Wedgwood dubbed his pottery "Queen's Ware," opened an exclusive showroom in London for a more affluent market, and pioneered sales practices of "money-back guarantees" and "free delivery."

Whether it has to do with livestock, pottery, or how we present ourselves online, branding is simply about *identity*. Personal branding simply expands branding to include a person's ideas, expertise, reputation, and personality. We intentionally craft a public identity for an express purpose.

During my adolescent AIM years, my express purpose was to get people to think I was cool. But is it really all that different today? Here we are all these years later podcasting, blogging, and spending countless hours on social media, presenting ourselves to the world for an express purpose. We want to gain more followers, attract attention, and maybe even make money.

But we've been doing this all wrong, and it's starting to catch up with us. People are getting tired of the constant noise.

They're tired of empty promises made by the latest internet millionaires. They're tired of image. They're tired of the lack of authenticity.

Much of the personal brand space plays out in two ways. The first group of people sells a false version of themselves, thinking that image or perception alone will get them the results they seek. These folks don't realize that attention isn't owed, it's earned. (Please don't be one of those people who rents a mansion on Airbnb, stages a photoshoot, and says it's their house.)

The flip side of presenting a false version of yourself is over-sharing in the name of authenticity. They talk nonstop about their issues, sometimes revealing way more than what is even comfortable to read about. It's as if these people are trying to sell their struggles, and it doesn't work in the long run. Like a car wreck, these folks garner attention, but it's short-lived.

So, what are we to do? Here's a simple question that can serve as a litmus test for you: "Can I build a campfire around what I'm sharing?" By this, I mean, is there warmth? Are you building something that is attractive and inviting to others? Can you build a community around it? Are you someone whom others want to invite onto their stages, in front of their employees, or into their lives?

You Already Have a Brand, So You Might as Well Become a Better One

The reality is that *you and I already have a brand*. We occupy an identity that varies depending on whom you talk to. Have you ever felt there is a difference between who you are at work vs. who you are at home or with your best friends? If so, it's because you have a particular identity among those different groups of people.

Your friends know you in a way your colleagues will never

know. Those same friends may have very little knowledge of who you are at work. Yet who you are at work vs. who you are at home is still... you.

But when you decide that you're going to build a business around yourself—a personal brand business—something shifts. Entrepreneurship has a funny way of bringing out the best in you while also revealing the roughest parts of you.

I want to level with you right off the bat. Don't build your brand; *become* your brand. Do the hard work required to become the person you're trying to sell to people. Embrace integrity. There is no shortcut.

When I was becoming my brand, there were areas in my life I had to do deep work in. There still are. But the process of building a warm, inviting campfire for others to gather around helped me get healthier... and become more successful. To this day, I find that the more I work on myself, the more money I make, and oddly enough—the less I care about the money. This is the kind of authenticity people are looking for.

All this talk of becoming a better person may seem like it's coming out of nowhere, but I assure you that you won't be on this journey very long before you have to confront your own dissonance if you want to go any further in this line of work.

Life Is Too Short for the Wrong Career

At times I'm asked, "How did you learn all this stuff about starting a personal brand business?" and the answer really comes down to confronting my own dissonance and building a life worthy of my own respect. The first time I was really confronted with this was in 2009.

On Father's Day that year, I flew cross-country to a 10,000+ member church in Colorado to meet with a pastor named Ross.

At the time, I was thirty years old and eighteen months into a position as the music director of a mid-sized church.

I reached out to Ross because I was hungry to be mentored by someone who was further along in the same role. He invited me to attend a conference he was hosting and agreed to meet with me one-on-one before the event. When I walked into his office, I was stunned. This guy was at the top of the mountain—figuratively because of his influence and literally because the back windows of his office offered a clear panorama of the Rockies!

Ross gave me some terrific insights during our time together, but an unexpected thing happened when I went back to my hotel that afternoon. I asked myself an innocent question that would forever change the course of my life: "If all goes well, do I want this guy's life in fifteen years?"

The answer was a resounding no.

That hit me like a ton of bricks. It wasn't until I met someone who was at the top of the mountain I was climbing that I realized: I was climbing the wrong mountain! There was simply no way I could, in integrity, admit that leading music for thirty minutes every Sunday morning for the same group of people was my life's calling. I wasn't living a life that I could genuinely respect for myself, and I realized: Life is too short for the wrong career.

Little did I realize my life would head down a completely unexpected path.

Highways vs. Off-Roading

Traditional career paths tell us that life is a highway or at least a corporate ladder. Everyone expects some curves or bumps, but for the most part, the path is pretty straightforward: Get a degree, get a job, consider an advanced degree, and work your way up the ladder.

The reality is that life isn't linear. Unfortunately, most of us are ill-prepared for that simple fact.

While society (and the hit Rascal Flatts song) tells us "life is a highway," real life is more like off-roading. I consider myself a decent driver, but you won't find me commandeering a Range Rover to off-road through the jungle. Off-roading requires a very different set of skills, and so does creating the life you want. Once you're out of school, no one tells you what books to read or what moves to make to advance to the next grade in life. You've got to figure it out for yourself, and that's when the comparison traps tend to set in.

If you're anything like me, we tend to look at other people and assume their path is straight and narrow, and ours is the only one that looks like a scrunched-up accordion. If you open your favorite GPS app and set the directions from New York City to San Francisco, the path looks like a straight shot right across the United States. But if you zoom into the starting point, you'll see the path to drive out of New York City alone will be more crooked than your least favorite politician.

As an inspirational meme on the internet once said, "Stop comparing your behind-the-scenes with someone else's highlight reel." So, where do we start?

Identifying Your Unique Expertise

One of the most clarifying exercises I did early on was to take inventory of what I did at work. In my mid-twenties, prior to my job as music director, I worked at an after-school academy preparing high school kids for their college entrance exams. (This is the same company I went back to several years later, where I was promoted to Chief Marketing Officer.)

One day I jotted down a short list of things I did in these roles, which looked something like this:

1.   I taught high school students.
2.   I spoke at church.
3.   I wrote songs.
4.   I led meetings for music team volunteers.
5.   I marketed the albums we recorded.
6.   I hosted conferences for the church.

Then it hit me. All I had to do was cross out the end of each of those sentences:

1.   I taught ~~high school students~~.
2.   I spoke ~~at church~~.
3.   I wrote ~~songs~~.
4.   I led meetings ~~for music team volunteers~~.
5.   I marketed ~~the albums we recorded~~.
6.   I hosted conferences ~~for the church~~.

When I saw those words staring back at me from my notepad, it was like I saw myself in a different light. More accurately, you could say I saw myself for the first time. For so much of our lives, we see ourselves through the lens of a company, organization, or role rather than the skills we possess or who we inherently are. We fail to see our unique expertise.

These mantras became a regular part of my self-talk early on: "I am a teacher! I am a speaker! I am a writer! I am a leader! I am a marketer! I am a conference host!" This was incredibly empowering, and I encourage you to do something similar.

Reinventing yourself is just as much about *changing the story you tell yourself* as it is in changing the story you tell the public.

I didn't realize it at the time, but I actually was rebranding myself... to myself.

There's a good chance you feel torn between the life you live vs. the life yet to be lived or feel weighed down by second-guessing, self-doubt, and frustration. This is normal, friend.

If you're going to be your own worst critic, you also have to learn how to be your own biggest fan. Be kind to yourself and do this inventory exercise. As you do so, the next step may surprise you.

This Is the Perfect Time to Go Silent

It's alright if you aren't sure what kind of business you want to start because there is still something very practical you can do to move forward: *Go silent* on social media.

Please don't misunderstand: I am not advocating that you completely shut down your social media activity. Rather, I encourage you to stop publicly reinforcing anything that has to do with your current or past career. That means no social media posts about how your day at work went, what you did at the office, or how much you hate your commute. The goal here is to create space in people's minds (and your own) so you can rewrite your life.

We see this phenomenon all the time in professional entertainment. Actor Steve Carell is most famous for his legendary role as Michael Scott on the classic comedy show *The Office*. Looking to reinvent himself, Carell left *The Office* (the show went on for several years after he left) and started to take serious dramatic film roles. Not long after, Carell was nominated for an Academy Award for his performance in the dark crime film *Foxcatcher*.

It would have made no sense for Carell to continue taking comedic roles while trying to establish himself in dramatic films.

He created space and distance between himself and *The Office* and ultimately changed the public's perception of him. You need to do the same.

Scroll back through your last thirty days' worth of posts on your favorite social network. Do they convey that you are an emerging expert in your new field? Or are they filled with updates about your job, pictures of your food, and posts about politics? Granted, these posts aren't wrong; they're just not helping you pivot right now.

You can't move on to the next chapter if you keep rereading the last one. Go silent for a bit and create that much-needed space.

The Only Three Markets We're Ever Really In

Once you create space, it's time to think about what general market you want to be in. It's likely that you are going to fall under one of the three broad areas of health, wealth, or relationships. For a more memorable take on this, I've also heard it said this way: People want to get paid, get laid, or live forever. Hilarious.

These categories are pretty self-explanatory. Tony Horton, creator of the famed P90X workout program, is clearly in the health industry. I spent two days working with Tony at his house a few years back for a marketing project and saw how much he genuinely cares about people's health. My friend Kristina Hoyer is a mindset and wellness coach who helped me get my nutrition on track. If you serve clients with meditation, yoga, spirituality, functional medicine, chiropractic, or even lifestyle planning, you're likely in this category as well.

As a business coach and marketing consultant, I fall under the wealth category. My job is to help businesses or individuals earn more money. Career coaches and executive leadership coaches are usually in this category as well because the client wants to perform better at work, raise the bottom line, or make more money.

If you are a marriage counselor, dating coach, or family counselor of any kind, you are in the relationship category. My good friend Susie Miller coaches high-level leaders in their relationships. Dr. Michelle Deering is a former client of mine who speaks primarily on the relationships mothers have with their daughters. Since our lives are driven by relationships, this is obviously a huge category.

I know that narrowing your focus can feel unsettling, like you're making a lifelong commitment to a particular market. I assure you that it's always possible to pivot later. Chalene Johnson was a fitness trainer who expanded her personal brand into online business coaching—she moved from health to wealth. Another good friend, Jamal Miller, started a membership site for single young adults offering relationship coaching and later extended his work into digital marketing under a different company. Jamal moved from relationships to wealth.

There's a reason we use the word "pivotal" to describe key turning points in life. I played basketball for my high school, and because I had a bit of height, my coaches always played me down low where I had to catch the ball near the basket and pivot to either shoot or pass. We worked a lot on planting my pivot foot in order to turn the rest of my body through the next move because I had to read the situation and didn't always know what I was going to do next.

Likewise, while it's possible for you to pivot later, it is vital you put roots down first, so if you decide to go in a different direction, you are able to move from a place of strength. Give some thought to which of these three general markets you fall into (health, wealth, or relationships) and you can always pivot later.

The 8-Step *Brand You Blueprint*

One of my biggest frustrations when starting out was trying to tie all the separate pieces of my fledgling business and brand together. There were plenty of terrific courses on speaking, blogging, selling, podcasting, and so forth, but I didn't know how they all fit together or which one I should work on first. I felt like Dr. Frankenstein, piecing together "random acts of marketing," hoping it would help me build the business and life I dreamed of. Instead, I ended up with a monster—an unfocused, expensive, and non-revenue-generating monster.

Throughout the rest of this book, I'm going to guide you through an 8-step framework I call the *Brand You Blueprint*. This blueprint isn't something I "created" as much as it was something that was revealed to me, both through my own journey and in working with my clients over the past seven years.

The key to the blueprint is that each step is built one on top of the other. If the previous step isn't clearly established, everything after it will eventually falter. Think of each of these steps like digits in a phone number: You can have the right digits, but if you don't put them in the right sequence, you won't be dialed in.

We will cover each of these steps in depth in the following chapters, but let's do a quick overview of each concept.

BRAND YOU BLUEPRINT

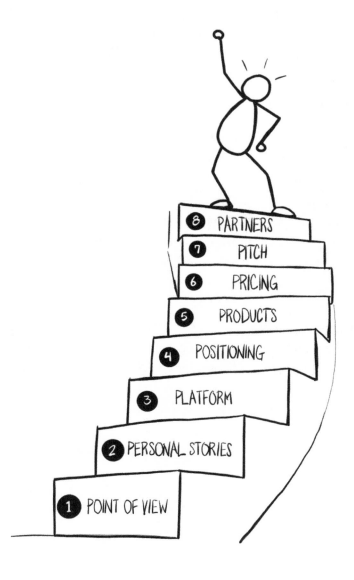

1. Point of View

There's only one place your message and brand can stem from if it's going to have a fighting chance: your core. We'll go through three simple questions to draw out what's really inside so you can establish a clear point of view that cuts through the noise. If you aren't living from your core and giving your fullest gifts, people will feel your lack of true purpose.

2. Personal Stories

Personal stories give context to who you are and why you do what you do. There are three stories you need to be able to tell at the drop of a hat, and these stories will stem easily from the work we do in the previous step. The good news? None of these stories are your *life* story, so you don't have to worry about writing your autobiography. These are simply stories that create connection with the market and differentiate you from the competition.

3. Platform

The third step is to build a platform for your brand to stand on, whether it be a blog, podcast, or social media channel. I mentioned earlier that many people build things out of order, and this is the first and most common place a breakdown occurs. You don't need to spend money on a snazzy logo or expensive website yet. In this chapter, we'll discuss what channels you should use, and you'll also learn why I chose to build my brand on some channels over others.

4. Positioning

Your positioning is determined most by where you sit relative to the competition. This is more than drawing a distinction between being a "high-end" vs. "mass market" brand. I'm going to show you a simple way to differentiate yourself and also give you some behind-the-scenes looks at how I leverage my positioning to open up new markets and opportunities.

5. Products

There is an old baseball movie starring Kevin Costner called *Field of Dreams* known for a famous line: "If you build it, they will come." That sounds like a nice premise, but when it comes to building products and services, it is completely false. It's hard to sell something that no one wants. I'm going to give you a few simple scripts you can use to validate what your market wants and then show you how to create a few products in a relatively short amount of time. You'll also learn the "five plays" of the most successful personal brands and how they tie into productization.

6. Pricing

I once heard professional speaker Ken Davis, founder of SCORRE, tell a story about one of his early lessons in business. Ken spoke at an event and was approached by a businessman interested in having him speak to his company. Ken was unsure about what to charge and lowballed his fee thinking it would get him the gig. The man replied, "Oh, I'm sorry. We only hire professionals." Ouch! This story shows you why it is so important to have the previous steps in the *Brand You Blueprint* built out. If you're clear on your positioning and products, your price becomes easier to determine. We'll cover a few simple strategies you can use to set your fees and prices.

7. Pitch

Not all sales pitches are equal: Some will be sent via email; others will be posted on a website, and depending on your business or product, you may need to close some deals on the phone or face-to-face. Since your sales pitch will vary from offer to offer, I will show you a few proven techniques that will remove the guesswork from selling.

8. Partners

As my friend Todd Herman says, "Relationships are rocket ships." Once you have the previous steps built out, you're in a prime position to attract partners who will help you get more exposure, grow your following, and even sell your products for you. I'm going to give you an inside look as to how strategic partnerships can skyrocket the growth of your business. If you stay the course and build some key relationships, there is no limit to what you can accomplish.

Success Is Sequential, Not Simultaneous

I've used the *Brand You Blueprint* with everyone from side-hustle startups to multi-million-dollar personal brand businesses. When a brand or product "fails to launch," it is often because there is a breakdown in one of the prior steps. Think about it:

1. If you build an online Platform with no Point of View or Personal Stories, you have no content for your website and no context for why your business exists.
2. If you haven't determined your Positioning, you won't know what kind of Product to create or how to Price it.
3. If you don't validate your offer, you won't know how to Pitch it or how to attract Partners who promote you.

It's important to understand this powerful concept I heard from Gary Keller, founder of the real estate empire Keller Williams: "Success is sequential, not simultaneous." You won't build your business overnight, but the *Brand You Blueprint* will guide you.

Who Do You Have to Become in Order to Serve the People You Want to Serve?

The years after my revelation in Colorado weren't always easy, but they were worth it. I look back on those early years with fondness because they made me who I am today and allowed me to share these insights with you. You're reading my story now, but one day you will tell the story you are living today, and someone else will benefit because of it. I promise you it will be worth it.

But before you can move on, you have to know where you are.

I challenge you to take these steps. Take inventory of what you do at work so you can start to see yourself in a different light. Push pause on any social media updates that reinforce what you are currently doing. Consider which general market you are in: health, wealth, or relationships. Then jot down some answers to this simple question: "Who do I have to become in order to serve the people I want to serve?" Do you need to become a better communicator? A more self-aware person? A leader? A risk-taker?

Even though it might be a bit uncomfortable, thinking through and writing out who you are and what you want is essential to becoming the person you're trying to sell to others. The credibility isn't in the teaching; the credibility is in the living.

Next, I'll tell you about the two types of entrepreneurs in the personal brand space and the Path ahead. Keep reading, and let's get a clearer picture of where you're going.

CHAPTER TWO

How-To-Preneur vs. Ideapreneur: Which One Are You?

Several years ago, my sister, Esther, recommended a book by Japanese author Marie Kondo called *The Life-Changing Magic of Tidying Up*. The premise of the book is to declutter your life by going through the items in your home. If an item "sparks joy" in you, you keep it. If the item doesn't invoke that kind of feeling, you thank the item for being a part of your life and release it (or as normal people call it, chucking it into the trash).

My reaction to Esther when she told me about the book was an incredulous, "Wait. Are you saying I'm dirty?!?" (Clearly, I did not think I had a problem that needed to be solved.)

You might argue that Kondo's book is about how to clean your house or declutter your life, but it's more than that. It's a philosophy of life. A book titled *How To Clean Your House* would be very practical and straightforward, but it wouldn't sell as well. Tidiness is very subjective, and it's nearly impossible to get someone to fork over hard-earned cash to fix a problem they don't think they have. That's the nuance (and brilliance) of Kondo's brand.

I talked earlier about how nearly all personal brand businesses fall into one of the three big markets: health, wealth, or relationships. Now it's time to consider which of the two types of entrepreneurs you are in your market. It's important to know the difference between the two because they monetize in very different ways, and both have distinct advantages and disadvantages. These are the two types:

1.   The *How-To*-Preneur
2.   The *Idea*preneur

1. The *How-To*-Preneur simply teaches people how to fix a problem or fixes it for them.

The advantage of a How-To-Preneur is that the problem they solve is very easily identified: Two of the most popular phrases that people type into internet search engines are "how to" or "how do I." The solution is usually a step-by-step or clearly defined pathway. The disadvantage of being a How-To-Preneur is that there is a ton of competition. Think of all the people out there who show others how to get fit, how to make more money, or how to have better relationships.

2. An *Idea*preneur has a particular message, perspective, or philosophy they are trying to spread.

The advantage of being an Ideapreneur is that there isn't much competition in the market because the idea is usually unique. The disadvantage is that most people won't easily understand your idea or, worse, aren't convinced they have a problem that needs to be solved. Moreover, an Ideapreneur may not always want to fix an actual problem at all. Often, they simply want to raise awareness about a particular issue.

For example, let's say you have two authors in a room. One is a How-To-Preneur and the other is an Ideapreneur. The How-To-Preneur will write a curriculum-based book (much like the one you are holding in your hands). The Ideapreneur will write a message-based book, like marketing guru Seth Godin's *Purple Cow*. The premise of *Purple Cow* is to put something phenomenal, counterintuitive, or unique into your products that stands out almost as conspicuously as, well, a purple cow. Yet nowhere in the book does Godin explain how to do that. His message to business owners is simply, "Go be remarkable!"

The brilliance of Kondo's book, which went on to be a best seller and a TV series, is that she is more of an Ideapreneur than a How-To-Preneur. Even if she is teaching people how to "spark joy" in their lives, her message is deeper than that. Her methods have roots in the national religion of Shintoism, and Japanese culture innately values minimalism. Her vision isn't to create clean homes; it's to help people live by a philosophy of tidiness and enjoy the calm mindset a decluttered life can inspire.

The Monetization Path

Many Ideapreneurs go astray because they try to build their business or expand their influence the same way a How-To-Preneur does.

As a How-To-Preneur, you can simply showcase your expertise and your ability to solve problems. If a prospect likes and trusts you, you can close a sale with relative ease. I am more of a How-To-Preneur. When personal brand businesses struggle with their marketing or sales, they contact me to fix the problem. I walk them through the *Brand You Blueprint*, dial in their marketing messages, and write high-converting sales pages and emails. It is a straightforward process.

As an Ideapreneur, there is an extra step in the sales conversion process because you have to convince a prospect there is a problem to begin with.

Let's go back to Marie Kondo and see if we can glean some insights from how she monetized her ideas. The book that put Kondo on the map, *The Life-Changing Magic of Tidying Up*, was first published in late 2010. Let's say that Kondo penned the book a year or two earlier. According to various interviews, Kondo was a cleaning consultant while she wrote the book. She was not the widely recognized brand she is today.

This is important because it's easy to say, "Look at Marie Kondo! All she had to do was write a book and BOOM—she blew up, got a TV series on Netflix, and became a global brand! I want that!" But consider how long her branding process took. Kondo had been consulting since she was in her mid-twenties. Her TV series didn't air until 2019, *eight years* after her book was published!

Whenever I advise aspiring Ideapreneurs, I tell them the story of Marie Kondo and ask kindly but directly: "Do you have the staying power to commit to this idea for that amount of time? Can you make ends meet financially in other ways while your ideas reach the market, if they do at all?" Patience is power. Unfortunately, most people aren't that patient!

As far as I can tell, Marie Kondo is doing quite well. The book and TV series garnered her plenty of publicity, and her company has created all kinds of branded products under the name Kon-Mari—including bins, stacking boxes, and wall organizers. (The irony of her advocating for a decluttered life while also selling a ton of products for your home is not lost on me.) She's written several more books, and you can even pay to become a KonMari certified cleaning consultant.

"Productization" of Kondo's philosophy didn't happen until much later in her career—her Path to success was not easy, and it certainly didn't happen overnight.

You may not care for productizing your ideas the way Marie Kondo has, so let's look at another Ideapreneur who has done something a bit different with her ideas: Dr. Brené Brown.

The Idea of Vulnerability

Most people know Brené Brown as a best-selling author, but most of her career has been as a researcher and university professor specializing in the study of courage, vulnerability, and shame. Dr. Brown had been quietly doing her work for years until her big break came in the form of a TEDx Talk in June 2010.

In her Netflix special, *The Call to Courage*, Dr. Brown recounts that her breakthrough was an "accident." The TEDx event took place at the University of Houston, where she was planning on giving a data-focused presentation on vulnerability, a subject she had been researching for years and a speech she had given several times before.

While flying to Houston, she decided to shift topics and talk about her own personal journey with vulnerability.

After delivering the speech, Dr. Brown felt uneasy because of how publicly vulnerable she was. She figured it was no big deal because there were only several hundred people in the room during her presentation, many of whom were colleagues.

To her surprise (and apparently, horror), her presentation went viral online. The video garnered millions of views but also attracted a swarm of internet trolls who made awful comments about her. While dealing with the emotional weight of the hate, Brown came across a speech by former American president Teddy Roosevelt, which inspired her book *Daring Greatly*.

> "It is not the critic who counts; not the man who points out how the strong man stumbles, or where the doer of deeds could have done them better. The credit belongs to the man who is actually in the arena, whose face is marred by dust and sweat and blood; who strives valiantly; who errs, who comes short again and again, because there is no effort without error and shortcoming; but who does actually strive to do the deeds; who knows great enthusiasms, the great devotions; who spends himself in a worthy cause; who at the best knows in the end the triumph of high achievement, and who at the worst, if he fails, at least fails while daring greatly, so that his place shall never be with those cold and timid souls who neither know victory nor defeat."
> —*Theodore Roosevelt*

Her book, *Daring Greatly*, went on to sell over two million copies and counting.

Eventually, Dr. Brown created a certification program based on her research called The Daring Way™, designed for work with individuals, couples, families, and groups. As her personal brand grew, her speaking and consulting fees likely increased. I should know; I tried to hire her on behalf of a client a few years ago!

Dr. Brown was able to raise awareness about a problem in a way that connected with people and allowed her ideas to spread. Most people don't wake up in the morning and say, "Today would be a great day for me to start living in a more daring way!" She educated the market about problems they don't often think about (vulnerability and shame) and then presented a solution.

At Their Own Pace and in Their Own Space

Whether you are a How-To-Preneur or an Ideapreneur, at some point it will be important for you to put your expertise into some kind of format (recorded video, audio, book, blog, etc.) so people can interact with your content in privacy—or as I like to say: at their own pace and in their own space. Let me elaborate.

I have several friends who are counselors. Every day, they walk their clients through incredibly challenging issues: addiction, divorce, trauma, and more. One of my counselor friends called me one day asking me for advice on whether she should create a virtual coaching group to help people navigate divorce. She had been following a number of online marketers talking about how much money could be made selling online courses, and she wanted to supplement her income and help more people. I told her to pump the brakes because this was a classic example of having the right intention but the wrong business model.

You may say, "But Mike, there is a clear problem that needs to be solved. Navigating divorce is a big deal!" Yes, but not every problem is solved in one particular way. There are reasons people going through a divorce do not buy online courses or join group coaching programs. It is an extremely private matter!

Imagine someone being on rocky terms with their spouse and running a $497 charge on their credit card to join a coaching group about divorce—only for their spouse to see the charge on their bank statement. (Good luck explaining that one.)

I went through a painful divorce several years ago and read about eight different books and watched countless videos online about the topic. I never would have purchased an online course or joined a coaching group. For me, the issue was way too personal.

When it comes to issues like divorce, addiction, abuse, mental health, daring greatly (and yes, tidying your house), these kinds of topics are usually better introduced to prospects by letting them consume the content at their own pace and in their own space.

What I suggested to my friend was she create "cornerstone content"—a signature speech, methodology, or framework that she could post online, publish in a small book, or teach on a podcast. This would be her particular approach toward helping people understand and navigate divorce. Her ideas would permeate the market, and she would grow an audience who would pay her not just for her services but for her products, which bear her signature framework.

This is exactly what happened, albeit inadvertently, with Brené Brown. Perhaps there were people who watched Dr. Brown's speech with a bunch of friends while scarfing down popcorn and beer, but I'm willing to bet most watched it alone. Many of those folks then read her books alone, listened to her podcasts alone, and felt like "Brené" (many of her most avid fans are on a seemingly first-name basis with her) was a silent friend through difficult stages in life. This is why most successful Ideapreneurs write books, host podcasts, or give speeches.

Success leaves clues. Let's reverse-engineer what we've seen from these two Ideapreneurs, Marie Kondo and Brené Brown.

What do they have in common?

1. They committed to their idea, perspective, or philosophy for an incredibly long time.
2. They found other ways to monetize their expertise while their ideas got out into the marketplace—Kondo was still consulting and Dr. Brown was still lecturing, consulting, and writing.
3. They put their ideas into a medium that allowed people to engage their ideas at their own pace and in their own space.
4. Their work was promoted on a much larger platform, helping them gain mass exposure—Kondo on Netflix and Brown on a TED Talk.

Let's take a breath here and recap a few of the things we should consider.

First, you should know which of the three general markets you are in: health, wealth, or relationships. (I would say that both Kondo and Dr. Brown are in the health and wellness markets—with Dr. Brown's work also touching the relationship space, since vulnerability plays a huge part in how we relate to others.)

Second, you should have a better idea of which one of the two types of entrepreneurs you are: a How-To-Preneur or an Ideapreneur. Now, we turn our attention to whether you have a vertical vs. horizontal focus.

The Two Types of Focus: Vertical or Horizontal

Some time back, I interviewed marketing expert Ilise Benun on my podcast and found her approach toward niching down really helpful. Benun prefers to frame markets through the word *focus* instead of the word *niche*, and it's a terrific way to look at things.

There are two types of focus when it comes to your business:

1. The Vertical Focus
2. The Horizontal Focus

The vertical focus has to do with a specific kind of client or industry.

Business folks use this terminology all the time—they just tend to abbreviate it and call it a "vertical." Consider a marketing firm whose tagline is "We help you do good, even better." Their vertical focus might be nonprofit organizations. This is still a very broad focus (there are hundreds of kinds of nonprofits), but it's clear they are only for nonprofits.

Marketing firms tend to offer a range of different services from logo design, website design, or social media advertising. These are all separate disciplines, but if you have a clear vertical focus, you can offer a wide number of products or "A-to-Z" services as a one-stop shop as long as you have the right people coming to you.

A horizontal focus has to do with an almost singular product or service you offer across a number of industries.

Perhaps you design websites across nearly all verticals. Maybe you offer freelance writing for nearly any kind of business. My friend Mark Stern launched a business that provides custom "swag" boxes with mugs, t-shirts, and booklets for nearly any kind of business event. He has a singular product across all kinds of verticals.

Early in my consulting career, my focus was simply "anyone who pays me." My client list reflected my lack of focus: a capital fundraising consultant, a public speaking trainer, a family law attorney, and even a high-end Beverly Hills oral surgery practice that had A-list celebrity clients. I felt like I had four different bosses because, well, I did.

Eventually, I wised up and zeroed in on one vertical focus: business thought leaders. My horizontal focus involved two things: brand strategy (I would advise them on marketing campaigns) or product launch copywriting (writing high-converting sales pages, ads, and other direct-response collateral).

When I narrowed my focus, my revenue shot through the roof, but more than that, I reclaimed my sanity.

When you cross-reference the horizontal and vertical focus, it's like the crosshairs on a scope: You know who to target and how to accurately reach them. Be patient with yourself because narrowing your focus is usually a longer process than any of us would prefer. Let me give you one more thing to consider because this was incredibly helpful to me.

Demographics vs. Psychographics

Early on in my side hustle (remember I was working full-time and figuring out what I wanted to do), I attended an out-of-town seminar about identifying your "avatar" or ideal client. The speaker asked us a bunch of unproductive questions like, "How old is your ideal client? How much money do they make? How many kids do they have? What car do they drive?" I thought this was a bunch of nonsense because it was too theoretical. Had I known the answers, I wouldn't have been sitting there!

To this day, I hate avatar exercises because you can't ask an aspiring entrepreneur who their ideal client is when that person doesn't yet know their own identity. Avatar exercises are fine if you have a more established business, but for those just starting out, they are frustrating at best.

The speaker at the seminar didn't understand the difference between demographics and psychographics. Avatar exercises are great for many retail businesses because their customers are generally defined by *demo*graphics: their age, sex, income, family situation, education, and more.

But in the personal brand space, many of us work with people based on *psycho*graphics: the classification of people according to their attitudes, aspirations, and other psychological criteria. In other words, dealing with people based on how they think.

On the flight home from the event, I whipped out my notebook determined to figure out who my ideal client was. There wasn't enough legroom in coach (I'm 6'3"), which probably sparked an even greater fire in me. I was cranky about all things—the conference, the lack of clarity in my business, and my knees literally pressing up against the seat in front of me. My thoughts began to flow, and in a rage of frustration, I scribbled down a few characteristics of my ideal client:

1. Someone who will take action
2. Someone who is willing to invest in themselves
3. Someone who is willing to take a risk
4. Someone who will not make excuses
5. Someone who does not view an investment as an expense or loss

In a moment of clarity, it hit me: The person I wanted to work with was *me*, two years prior.

Two years earlier, I had quit my music director job in Connecticut, stopped listening to gossip for men (also known as sports talk radio) during my commutes, and devoured business and leadership podcasts instead. Instead of sports magazines, my shelves started to fill up with books about marketing, entrepreneurship, and personal development. I used my vacation days to attend conferences in order to grow my network and learn new things. (I met most of the folks who endorsed this very book at those conferences.)

When you invest in yourself, the game is in your favor because you dictate the returns. Here you are, reading this book, learning, growing, and investing time and money into your own development. Wouldn't you like to work with someone like that? You may be your own ideal client. And if there is one of you, there are more of you—hundreds, thousands, tens of thousands, and even millions.

If you've been frustrated trying to figure out your ideal client, consider looking at the market through the lens of psychographics. After all, you will often find twenty-three-year-olds at a personal development seminar sitting right alongside a seventy-three-year-old.

That's not to say that demographics and psychographics are mutually exclusive. You may want to work with growth-minded twenty-somethings or seventy-somethings who want to write a book. My friend Dana Malstaff, founder of Boss Mom, helps mothers "raise babies and businesses." Clearly there is a crossover in Dana's audience between demographics and psychographics. My point is that we tend to overlook the latter. I cannot overstate how mind-blowing this realization was to me at the time.

The Path of the Personal Brand

One of the most unique (and challenging) things about building a personal brand business is that you can't just "buy" one. You can't go on eBay or Craigslist and acquire someone's influence. You can't "buy" Marie Kondo or Brené Brown, even if you were to acquire the rights to their intellectual property, customer databases, and social media accounts. When building a personal brand business, everyone starts from zero.

When I ask people why they want to start a personal brand business, many respond by citing influential people who seem to live in a magical place, which I've since dubbed "The Land of Whatever I Want."

Often they will cite people like Dwayne "The Rock" Johnson, Oprah, Gary Vaynerchuk, or Joe Rogan, who can seemingly make money doing whatever they want. What most people don't understand is that there is a Path to the place of influence these folks and others have reached, but it requires walking through a lonely place I call the "Valley of Focus." Allow me to explain.

Let's say you start your journey by writing blog posts, sharing inspirational quotes on social media, or starting a new podcast. Unfortunately, it doesn't really seem like anyone is listening. (This is normal.) Your friends, family, and colleagues are a bit confused by what you're doing and some may even stop following you online. You feel more alone than ever. Welcome to the Valley of Focus, friend.

In the Valley of Focus, you whittle down all of your random ideas to focus on one idea, topic, or market. You decide whether you will specialize in health, wealth, or relationships. You narrow your focus even further to determine what you will do in your particular market. It hurts because you are multi-passionate, but

you also start to understand, much like a dance club, that you cannot play five different types of music and expect to attract patrons to your establishment. (Ballroom music and heavy metal just don't mix well.)

When I started to focus on business and marketing, the vast majority (my guess is about 90%!) of the people who I knew through my music director position stopped following me online. I simply wasn't relevant to them anymore. I had to make a decision: Do I keep going on this Path, or do I change my mind?

As your focus becomes more narrow, something interesting happens: You become known for a few things, then eventually for just one or two things. This attracts other influential people who have followings of their own. An influential person may hire you or ask you to speak to their audience about your area of expertise. As a result, some of their followers start following you.

Another influencer, seeing your connection to the first influencer, assumes you are legitimate and asks you to speak to their audience, and BAM—the process repeats itself and you've gained a few more followers! You continue to grow and become a rising star, all while building an engaged audience.

Over time, your audience keeps following you not just because of what you know but because of who you are. Again, you aren't just building a brand, you are *becoming* your brand. You are, as I mentioned earlier, building a campfire that people can gather around.

Because you have focus, the quality of your work improves. Your expertise becomes established, and people's lives are transformed because of you. Your biggest fans become superfans who will gladly follow you into nearly any of your future pursuits. If you have enough of these folks, they will help you reach "The Land of Whatever I Want"—and stay there.

"The Rock" Can Do Anything, Right?

Dwayne "The Rock" Johnson is one of this generation's biggest action stars, but for decades he was a professional wrestler. That was his Valley of Focus. Lest you think he was always a success, Johnson originally wanted to be a football player but never made it to the NFL. His childhood dream shattered, Johnson pivoted into professional wrestling (his father and grandfather were also wrestlers) and eventually became one of the industry's biggest stars, known as The Rock.

Johnson slowly started to land a few movie roles because of his popularity in wrestling. When he left the industry to pursue acting full-time, many wrestling fans felt he "sold out." Not all of them were thrilled he was acting, but enough of them did so that his movies did well. The rest is history: The Rock went on to star in big budget movies like *The Fast and the Furious* and *Jumanji*. He leveraged his huge following on social media to showcase his workouts, which landed endorsements with athletic apparel company Under Armour and even (of all things) his own brand of tequila.

Yes, it seems The Rock can do whatever he wants, but his rite of passage was spending decades in the wrestling ring after failing to make it as a professional football player. He wasn't an immediate star in professional wrestling either—go online to watch his early matches, and you'll quickly see that most fans initially hated him. No one could have imagined he would become one of the industry's biggest stars and then, eventually, one of the most recognizable celebrities in the world.

The other influential people I mentioned earlier also walked the Path through the Valley of Focus. Oprah Winfrey started out as a co-anchor for the local evening news. Gary Vaynerchuk sold wine for years in relative anonymity before becoming a social media star. Joe Rogan was a TV host and mixed martial arts commentator, garnered a following, and went on to host one of the most popular podcasts in the world where he seemingly talks about (you guessed it) whatever he wants.

Keep Walking the Path

You may not want to be as big of a name as the people I mentioned or even be in a position where you can do "whatever you want." But it's important to understand the long game of building a personal brand business. As you can see, many people (even noncelebrities) have walked this Path. The issue isn't fame; the issue is focus.

The key right now is to narrow your focus so you attract clients who come to you for a particular purpose. After some time, you may attract a following, and as your relationship grows with those people, a small percentage of them may follow you into any new venture.

As we head into the first step of the *Brand You Blueprint*, realize that clarity comes in shades and nuances. It won't come all at once, but it will come. For now, consider whether you are a How-To-Preneur or an Ideapreneur. Do you prefer a horizontal focus, a vertical focus, or a blend of both? Does differentiating between demographics and psychographics provide some more clarity for you?

Now you know what the Path requires of you. It won't be easy. You will be challenged. But if you're game to keep going, let's take the first step of the *Brand You Blueprint*: your Point of View.

PART TWO

The Brand You Blueprint

8 PARTNERS
7 PITCH
6 PRICING
5 PRODUCTS
4 POSITIONING
3 PLATFORM
2 PERSONAL STORIES
1 POINT OF VIEW

CHAPTER THREE

Point of View:
The PB3

In my first job in sales and marketing, I got paid to lie.
Seriously.

During my sophomore year in college, I took the spring semester off because I couldn't pay for school. The plan was to find work that would also look better on my resume than busing tables at a New Jersey diner.

Back then, people looked for jobs in the Sunday newspaper, and one week I came across a listing for a part-time telemarketing position. Sales never appealed to me, but the ad said they would train me, pay an hourly base rate, and pay a commission on every sale. The money seemed good, and to my surprise, I was pretty good on the phone. My name was routinely in the "Top Three" leaderboard every day.

Unfortunately, all I did was flat-out lie. If there was ever a scenario where the higher-ups believed the end justified the means, this was it. I was encouraged to lie, trained to lie, and expected to lie, all for the sake of the sale.

The company I was working for sold an industrial cleaning detergent to factories. Our prospects were factory foremen whose names were collected on cards at various trade shows throughout the country. (That was probably a lie; the company most likely bought a mailing list, but that's what I was told.)

There was a process and script I was to follow, without question. I'd dial up a factory and claim I was returning a call from the foreman. If he came on the line, I would ask if he wanted us to fulfill his request to send a sample of our product.

The bewildered foreman would often reply, "I don't remember asking for a sample," and my scripted response was, "Maybe one of your employees or colleagues gave us your information at a trade show thinking you would find this useful." Then I'd pitch the product.

If he ordered, I would claim that my fax machine was broken, tell him I had to walk to a different fax machine across the office to receive his order, and ask him to fax it to me while he was still on the phone. In reality, we wanted him to fax the order right away because it would be too easy for him to ignore the fax later.

Even my name became a lie! After the third time some foreman pronounced my last name "King" instead of "Kim," I just went with it and called myself Michael King. It's not like many of the places I was calling ever saw a Korean guy anyway; these folks were scattered all throughout rural America. Michael King actually sounded pretty cool, as if I were one of Leonardo DiCaprio's sales sharks in *The Wolf of Wall Street*. Maybe that's how I made so many sales.

I didn't stay at the job very long because apparently beneath my hardened emotional exterior lies a deep sense of right and wrong. Apparently not lying to people is one of my core values. It's why I quit that job, and it's why I am going to be brutally honest as we start going through the *Brand You Blueprint*.

I love what good branding and marketing can do for you, but I also hate that the kindest people and sharpest minds all too often get left behind simply because they aren't as good at it as others. I hate that great products and services get passed over because their creators aren't willing to have a team of college sophomores lie about fax machines in order to make sales. And I hate that I'm starting to feel a tinge of embarrassment when I tell people I am a marketer, not because I'm embarrassed of the profession but because the profession is starting to become so icky.

Half-truths, fudging of the facts, and blatant lies are everywhere. Untold amounts of people are forking over the equivalent of an annual college tuition for courses that don't really set them free but rather create an unhealthy codependency on the guru who created them.

This mini-rant is more than just how I feel about things it is actually the first step in the *Brand You Blueprint:* **your Point of View**. Voicing (or even having) your own opinion might seem unsettling at first, but if you're going to start a business based on who you are, you might as well base it on something you're passionate about. There are endless other ways to make money if you just want to make money. Open a restaurant. Flip properties. Do weird things online.

This line of work is different. Being an entrepreneur is hard enough, but if what you do day in and day out doesn't stem from a deeper place within you, you won't last.

To help draw out what's inside, I use three simple questions that I call the Personal Brand 3, or PB3 for short. (And yeah, I'm from Jersey, so please excuse the salty language.)

1.   What pisses you off?
2.   What breaks your heart?
3.   What's the big problem you're trying to solve?

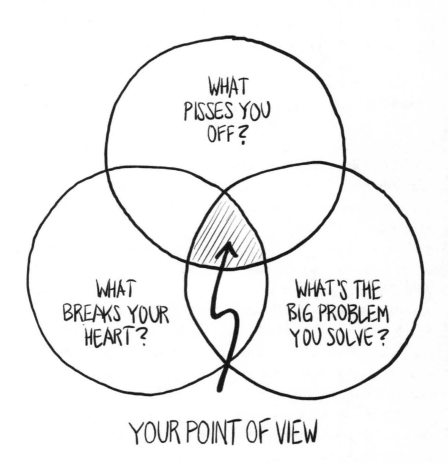

Question 1 is about the injustice you see in the world. Question 2 is about the compassion you carry inside. Question 3 is the purpose of your business.

The intersection of these three things is where your point of view is found:

To put it bluntly: Find a problem that pisses you off, figure out how to fix it, and get paid to fix it. In its simplest form, *business is nothing more than solving a problem for a profit.* But branding is more complex, especially in the personal brand space.

Most of us think that simple and clear messaging is enough for us to cut through the noise. This is a half-truth because while that may be true for other businesses, it's not true in a personal brand business.

Imagine walking up to a speaker after you hear a riveting, life-changing speech and asking her, "Why did you get into speaking?"

She responds, "I sort of believe in what I shared, but I'm really just doing this to make money." Yuck, right?

You may say, "Mike, I'm not looking to overthrow a government, start a new religion, or transform an industry. I just want to quit my life-sucking day job." That's fine for now, but if you're going to achieve long-term success in this line of work, you need a point of view.

When you have a minute, go back and consider how I wrote the opening sections of this very chapter. The telemarketing story frames my love of marketing but also how I hate that good people are passed over because they struggle with marketing. I used the word *hate* intentionally to convey what pisses me off, and this book is my attempt to solve that problem for you. The context (my story) frames the content (the tips I share with you in this book). It's like the old saying goes: Content is king, but context is the kingdom.

Let's dive a bit deeper so you have a concrete example of how to use the PB3 for your own purposes. I'm going to share quite a bit more of my own journey here, but this is because I want you to have an example of how to use the PB3 to your benefit.

Tipping Point

In 2013, my mother, sister, and brother-in-law came to my condo for Thanksgiving. This was the first time I hosted Thanksgiving, and I was really excited about everyone coming over. By 1 a.m. the others fell asleep, so my mom and I started drinking deep into the night (as good Koreans are apt to do). This was the first time I had ever thrown back shots with Mom, and wow—the stories just started flying out of left field. I've cleaned up her broken English to make it, well, readable for you:

> "Michael, when I was a teen in Korea, my sister and I took our father's whisky out of the cabinet after he fell asleep, snuck out of the house, ran down the street to our friend's house, and we all got drunk together. Then we returned the bottle empty, and he just thought he drank it!"

> "Michael, one night when you were a baby, some friends came over to visit. You were crying because you were teething, so your father rubbed whisky over your gums, and you fell right asleep for the whole night! We were worried because you turned red, but you survived, so it's okay. The first time you ever got drunk was when you were a baby!" (Side note: What the…?)

> "Michael, when I was young, there were no dating sites, so the only way we met people were blind dates. One of our friends went on a blind date, but she was scared to go alone, so a few of us went to the restaurant where she was going and sat on the other side to spy on them. A very hairy, short man waddled in, and he looked like a panda bear, so we nicknamed him Panda-Oppa ("oppa" means older brother in Korean). She just laughed the whole night, and the next year she quit

school, married Panda-Oppa, and disappeared! That's how we dated back then—just marry a good guy who makes you laugh and is nice to you. They are still together and so happy!"

You can imagine my reaction to this conversation: complete and utter shock at realizing my mother ever did anything bad, tons of laughter, and deep gratitude that I somehow survived childhood. I also could have stayed up for hours drinking with her, but there was one small problem. I had to go to work the next day, Black Friday.

At the time, I was working as the Chief Marketing Officer for an educational company just outside of New York City. It really pissed me off that I had to go into work that day and leave my family at my own house while I drove an hour north to go to the office.

All kinds of thoughts ran through my head. What if my mother got into a car accident on her way home? What if this was the last day I would ever have these kinds of conversations with her? Why is someone else determining what days I'm allowed to spend with my loved ones? Wasn't pouring in sixty hours a week at work enough?

It wasn't enough because I never decided it was enough. Have you ever noticed how people rarely say "no" on your behalf when it comes to doing more work? This became an injustice to me, and I was insanely motivated to build my business and never let anyone control when I was allowed to spend time with my loved ones. Within eighteen months, I quit that job and went into business for myself full-time.

Whenever I'm asked about why I started my business, this Thanksgiving story is the one I tell. I've shared it on podcasts, interviews, and stages, and many people tell me this story is what they resonate with most. It is everywhere in my marketing—keynotes, webinars, social media, and yes, this book. This story is one of the things that frames my point of view on business and life.

The next thing that frames my point of view is the second question: "What breaks your heart?"

What Breaks My Heart

About a year after I went into my own business full-time, my friends Jason Clement and Jody Maberry were in town to help me with a business conference. The morning of the event, we drove down one of the longest roads in northern New Jersey: Kinderka-mack Road. It stretches across a number of different towns, and on any weekday morning, you will see bus stop after bus stop along the way full of people heading to work.

It was a miserable, rainy day, and I remember saying something like, "Guys, we're so lucky to do what we love. My heart breaks for the people waiting for the bus in this awful weather. I bet most of those folks don't really enjoy their job. There is probably a ton of wisdom, knowledge, and insight at that bus stop, but the world at large won't benefit because they're stuck in the grind. They go to work miserable, come home exhausted, steal a few moments with their families, sleep, and repeat the cycle day after day. The world is not a better place because of this!"

This wasn't an entitled, judgmental, or condescending comment. I said it because I lived it for so many years. Back then, there was a popular TV show about zombies called *The Walking Dead*, and it struck me that so many of us go through life like zombies. It's heartbreaking.

When I was working that earlier marketing job at the educational company, I'd often have conversations with coworkers about what they really wanted to do with their lives. These were some of the smartest people I knew—graduates from Cooper

Union, Columbia, and every other top university out there. They just didn't believe they had it in them (or were even allowed) to do anything different.

I had many conversations during those years with coworkers and high school students about creating the life they really wanted. Through the magic of social media, I occasionally hear from some of my former students. They're all grown up now—some have become doctors, others have started businesses, a few are even married. They tell me they still remember "life conversations" we often had and were grateful they knew at least one person who told them to do what they wanted with their life and not what someone else told them. I suppose I'm doing the same thing with you in this book. I want you to live the life you want.

The Walking Dead story conveys my compassion for the people I serve and frame my point of view. If I share these stories during any kind of presentation or marketing materials, they are usually followed by remarks about how many people aren't happy at work and why it's so important to do work you love and believe in.

What Is the Big Problem I'm Trying to Solve?

Now that you are starting to frame your point of view, you may be tempted to hire a marketing consultant to come up with some catchy slogan for your website or business card. I strongly advise against that. In other words, just don't!

I specifically mention slogans because I've been surprised at how many people ask for help with their slogan, as if some kind of catch phrase will magically set them apart from the competition. Slogans are not inherently valuable. Rather it is the context in which that slogan is expressed that gives it meaning.

One of the most popular slogans of our generation is Nike's "Just Do It." Take that same slogan and slap it onto the front window of a donut shop or skydiving company, and you completely change the message without changing a single word. Remember, content is king, but context is the kingdom.

For me, in "slogan speak," I simply say that my company exists to help people start, run, and grow a profitable personal brand business. That's the big problem I'm trying to solve. When I have the liberty to use a few more words, I say, "I teach an 8-step Blueprint to help you showcase your unique expertise and build a highly profitable, personally fulfilling business." Wordsmithed even further, the last thing I say on my podcast episodes for years has been: "Live your message, love your work, leave your mark on the world."

None of these one-liners were born from sitting around trying to think of a clever slogan. I've wasted plenty of hours trying to come up with a good one. They came from forming my point of view, creating content over many years, and helping clients.

I highly doubt anyone has hired me solely because of these one-liners. Rather, they hire me because I have a clear point of view on branding and marketing. They hire me because I've created content that establishes me as an expert. They hire me because they like my personality. They hire me because I get results.

When you look at your answers to the PB3, you might be surprised at what you find. I was.

After some time, I revisited my own answers to the PB3 and experienced a big shift in perspective for my business.

I never said, "You know what pisses me off? Really bad advertising!"

I never said, "You know what breaks my heart? Ugly websites and the Comic Sans font!" There are people who wake up in the morning and actually do get really pissed off about bad advertising. You can find them working at advertising agencies or freelancing, like my friend and designer, Jason Clement. These folks are right where they belong, and the world is a better place because people like Jason are in their sweet spot.

I realized my business was much deeper than marketing or branding. Going back through the PB3 helped me realize I was more than a marketer. I was (dare I say it?) more like a life coach who happens to help people become entrepreneurs and market themselves. This sparked a hotter motivation to double down on helping people start and grow a personal brand business.

Forming your point of view through the PB3 is simply about being honest with yourself. I spent way too many years burying my real desires in the name of being "content with what I have." It's possible to be grateful for what we have and still want something different. When you double down on gratitude at the expense of your own honesty, you really have a false gratitude that moves you out of integrity.

Life works because of tension. Light and dark. Good and evil. Pleasure and pain. I consider myself a compassionate guy, and I'm all for encouragement and positive reinforcement. But we can't deny that conflict, pain, and friction are incredible catalysts. Without friction between your tires and the road, your car isn't going anywhere. Friction is your friend. This is why I'm asking you, "What pisses you off?"

But how do we navigate that when it comes to making a change as big as our vocation or changing our brand identity?

Introducing the Sadistic Selfie

I'm going to admit that this is a purely Mike Kim invention. I've never heard of this being done, and I'm confident this odd strategy could only originate from my own twisted mind. I call it the Sadistic Selfie.

I cooked this up while I was working the marketing job I've been telling you about. Keep in mind, I was grateful for my job. I was making good money, well-respected in the company, and I learned invaluable lessons during my time there.

I was also totally miserable at times. I started taking selfies (privately) during those moments to remind myself that I wasn't all that happy:

Just look at that picture. I hope to one day have the honor of it being displayed in the Metropolitan Museum of Art's "Modern Lifestyle" exhibit. I've titled it, "The 4 Stages of Death by Conference Call."

These snapshots continued to serve as the reminder I needed to stay on track and keep going every time I felt like giving up on launching my own business. I had a whole folder of them on my phone. Every time I felt lulled into settling with my job, I opened my "Sadistic Selfies" folder and gave those pics a real good look. I intentionally did this after our really fun company holiday parties because they had a way of subtly luring me back into the grind. I'd find myself thinking, "Well, this isn't all that bad. I should be grateful I have this job!" and then whip out my Sadistic Selfies.

Though I've been full-time in my own business for many years now, I still use this tactic when I'm doing some sort of life-sucking task, like anything with technology, budgeting, or bookkeeping. It's helped me hire the right help and stay in my lane.

As a wise man once said, "There are two things in life that motivate you: the fear of pain and the desire for pleasure." Snap those pics, friend.

The Power of Contrast

Perhaps you think I'm a negative person after all my talk of sadistic selfies, friction, and asking you what pisses you off. What I'm really trying to do is help you get clarity through contrast. Contrast helps you gain clarity, identify things, and stand out. (This is one of the reasons I never wear black when speaking onstage. Most stages have black backdrops. It's hard to stand out when you blend in with the background.)

If your car is stuck in the snow and you don't have a shovel, what do you do? You drive forward, then backward, forward, then backward, all while turning the wheel in an effort to catch traction somewhere on the road. If your energy flows in only one direction all the time, you'll often end up just spinning your wheels.

Opposites create contrast that can lead to powerful breakthroughs.

An example:

1. Original Answer: It pisses me off that someone else determines what days I'm allowed to spend with my family.
2. Opposite: I'm starting this business because I believe I should have personal ownership of my freedom, time, and future—and believe other people should have the same.

So, what pisses you off? What breaks your heart? What is the big problem you're trying to solve? Your answers to the PB3 will form the basis for your personal stories.

Have fun with this and realize that it is normal to feel a bit foggy. Clarity comes through a marriage of movement and meditation, so we might as well get comfortable with the dance.

CHAPTER FOUR

Personal Stories:
Never Be "Blender Gray"

When I was a kid, my mother got swept up in the home juicing craze. The Juiceman was one of the original juicers, promoted on everything from late-night infomercials to magazines and talk shows. Sometime later, fitness guru Jack LaLanne released a competing product he called the Power Juicer, leveraging the power of his personal brand to make his juicer stand out.

I still remember Jack LaLanne performing an inordinate amount of pullups on TV, claiming he could do them in his seventies because he juiced (with his particular juicer, of course).

That's the power of a personal brand! The personal brand can get people to do (or buy) things they wouldn't otherwise do if just associated with a nameless, faceless thing. There were a number of Jack LaLanne fitness clubs around our neighborhood, so when it came down to purchasing a juicer, you can be sure my mother picked the Power Juicer. She was already familiar with the Jack LaLanne brand and had seen him on TV numerous times.

I will never forget the first time my mother made me some juice and forced me to drink it before I went to school. I was probably about ten years old, and I still remember how nasty that stuff tasted. I'm not quite sure what Mom put in the juice that day. Beets? Radishes? Lettuce? Spinach? Moss from our backyard? The color of the juice was a peculiar gray shade with a tiny hint of brown and green. I'm sure there were good nutrients inside, but it tasted horrible, and it wasn't very appealing.

I was always trying to find a way to describe that color until one day I heard my friend Sean Pritzkau use the term "blender gray." That was it! I now refer to the color of that juice as "blender gray," and there's one more branding lesson we can glean from all this talk about juicing. "Blender gray" is exactly how our brands look if we're not intentional about using personal stories in our marketing.

Personal Stories Keep You from Being Blender Gray

The reason personal stories are so important to your brand is that they make you stand out from the crowd. Your stories are, in essence, your unique selling proposition. No one can compete with them.

Take a stroll through the personal development section of your nearest bookstore. Are the messages really all that different? Are the messages of those books dramatically unique from one another? I'm positive there are some great titles on those shelves, but what really makes one book stand out from another is *the person who wrote them.*

As I've said, if I could sum up everything I feel about marketing in one sentence, it would be this: *Marketing isn't about closing a sale; it's about opening a relationship.*

Personal stories allow you to do exactly that. The personal stories I've shared with you so far have given you context for why I wrote this book and why I'm so passionate about my work. Having a few personal stories in your arsenal will do the same thing for you.

The Everyday Way to Craft a Personal Story

Before we get into the types of personal stories you can use in marketing, it's best to take a quick look at how to craft them. It's easy to assume that great storytelling is a talent reserved for the greatest orators or writers, but storytelling is more natural than we think. This is an easy but important framework to have in mind, adapted right from the Greek philosopher Aristotle's study of dramatic structure and storytelling:

INTRODUCTION   INCITING INCIDENT   RESOLUTION

Any good story involves a character who experiences an inciting incident that sets the rest of the tale into motion. We often get in our own way when writing stories because we get into "writing mode," and it's no surprise. For most of our lives, we were taught in school to write essays, not write stories. When we share stories in real life, we naturally start at the inciting incident. Let's say a loved one asks you how work was. You might say something like:

1. "You'll never guess what that idiot Mike Kim did in today's meeting! Ugh!"
2. "When I was getting out of the car this morning, I dropped my phone and it broke!"
3. "While I was headed out the door, my boss pulled me into the office and asked me point-blank how much I want to be paid to be Chief Marketing Officer of the company!"

One of my favorite kinds of TV programs are videos of animals in the wild, like those old *National Geographic* shows. Even those videos tell stories. A zebra is out grazing like any other normal day and all of a sudden—BAM!—he is surrounded by a pack of hungry, vicious hyenas. That is certainly an inciting incident.

The inciting incident is crucial to storytelling. If you've ever heard someone tell a story over dinner and thought to yourself, *Hurry up and get to the point*, it is probably because they're taking too long to get to the inciting incident.

The Three Types of Personal Stories

There are generally three kinds of stories you need in your marketing arsenal, and none of them need to be terribly in-depth. A word of relief: A personal story is not your *life* story.

Many people overthink storytelling because they think a

personal story means writing an autobiography. Good news: That is not necessary! In most cases, your clients and customers won't be interested in your life story—they just want a few insights into your background, why you do what you do, and whether you can solve their problems. Here are the three personal stories I recommend you start with:

1. The Founder Story
2. The Business Story
3. The Customer Story

1. The Founder Story: What Pisses You Off? What Breaks Your Heart?

The key to writing your Founder Story is to simply use the answers to the PB3 questions, "What pisses you off?" and "What breaks your heart?"

My friend and fundraising consultant Mary Valloni does this to great effect in her marketing. If you spend any time at all with Mary, you will quickly discover what pisses her off and breaks her heart: people and causes missing out on the help they need because the nonprofits that serve them struggle to raise money.

Mary writes,

> My senior year of college at the University of North Dakota, I took an internship with my college ministry overseeing their fundraising efforts, and I raised my own personal support. It was then that I realized how much I loved fundraising!
>
> I grew up in a large family (the youngest of seven kids!), and I learned quickly the value of working hard and being creative to raise funds for the organizations and activities I was a part of. Coming from a big family, there was no way my parents could pay for everything that all of us wanted to do. I raised funds to participate and travel

with my club soccer team, school conferences and competitions, and mission trips.

While I didn't end up a professional soccer player or a career missionary, the skills I learned selling candy bars and writing support letters have been integral in how I help individuals and organizations launch new, results-driven fundraising campaigns today.

I had the incredible honor of leading the fundraising efforts for some of the largest and most well-respected charitable organizations in the U. S. from 2001–2014 (American Cancer Society, ALS Association, and Special Olympics). Those years were transformational not only for me but for the organizations I worked with, as we increased revenue by tens of millions of dollars!

This is Mary's Founder Story—it is why she loves fundraising and why she worked for years on staff at various organizations.

2. The Business Story: What's the Big Problem You're Trying to Solve?

Your business story illustrates the "why" behind your actual company—even if you are a solo entrepreneur. You can feature the story of how you started your website, or your podcast, or your consulting practice. You can also use this kind of story to give context to why you created a certain product, program, or service.

The easy way to tell your Business Story is to take your answer to the PB3 question, "What is the big problem you're trying to solve?" and combine it with an inciting incident. Here's a portion of Mary's business story. The inciting incident will be very apparent to you:

The summer of 2013, while working for the American Cancer Society, my life drastically changed when I lost my dad to cancer. For the first time, I was faced with the possibility that my days could be numbered too. That next year, I resigned from my full-time fundraising career to start my entrepreneurial journey as a fundraising consultant.

> In 2014, Mary Valloni Consulting was born and has resulted in tens of thousands of lives being impacted through my work as a fundraising coach, my #1 Amazon Best Selling and award-winning book, *Fundraising Freedom*, and my top 10 Apple podcast on fundraising, *The Fully Funded Podcast*.

It takes a great deal of courage to talk about such a loss so openly, but that's precisely why Mary's story works. It all flows naturally because it is authentic and comes from the core.

The flip side would be the same old marketing jargon every other person uses: "I'll help your organization bridge the gap from where you are to where you want to be" or "I'll help you gain clarity on how to level up your business, career, and life." There is nothing wrong with those lines, but without personal stories, those slogans are just blender gray. Because she based her stories on inciting incidents, Mary cuts through the noise.

Please understand that the inciting incident in your story does not need to be a catastrophic event. Sometimes the inciting incident can be as simple as watching an inspirational clip from a video or a comment made in passing that sticks with you and becomes a catalyst for change.

In Mary's Founder Story, the inciting incident was simply volunteering to fundraise for her local college ministry. That wasn't a very flashy moment. In her Business Story, the inciting incident happened to be much more serious, but both play an important role in her message. The point is to make your story revolve around the inciting incident, whatever it may be.

In 2018, Mary and I started a training company together called Fully Funded Academy (FullyFundedAcademy.com) to help nonprofits raise more money by training their teams. When we launched, we made sure to tell that company's Business Story—Mary and I met at a conference through a mutual friend, sat down and mapped out an entire business plan on the back of the conference manual, and hosted our first workshop four months later.

To this day, our clients always want to know how we ended up meeting and working together. What they're really looking for is connection. They want to know that our friendship and partnership is solid, that we make a great team, and that they can trust us. Our Business Story conveys the feeling that we were almost destined to work together.

You can bet that every year we do a "business birthday" promotion to our market to celebrate our clients and pitch special offers.

By the way, if you run or are part of a nonprofit, the Business Story is very important. I've said repeatedly that business is simply solving a problem for a profit. However, there are some problems that are *not* profitable to solve—which is why we need nonprofits!

If you are in the nonprofit space, your version of the Business Story is simply your organization's story. How did your nonprofit start, and what is the problem you are trying to solve? You might be surprised at how much of a connection sharing those details can create with donors.

3. The Customer Story

The Customer Story is simply a transformation story of someone you've worked with. The following is a customer story by a former coaching client, Matt, that I used in a promotion for one of my marketing programs. Matt joined my program and came out of the gate swinging. He started a business in a completely new niche—and monetized within the first few weeks of our working together.

Matt's inciting incident will be very obvious:

> After ten years at my job, I went to work one typical Tuesday. At 10:30 a.m., I was given a severance package and basically being shown the door. I had to call a cab because I had to clear my desk and couldn't carry the boxes on my bike.
>
> I remember it was the prettiest day of the year. The sun was shining off the building. It was only 10:30 in the morning; the next thing you know I'm back at home asking, "Now what? What am I going to do?"
>
> I went to visit a friend of mine. He asked if the company gave me a severance package, and when I said yes, he got this big smile on his face and said, "So, they're funding your startup!"
>
> That was such a big shift for me; this idea that I wasn't let go and rejected but was actually given an incredible opportunity and a runway for a pivot.
>
> Here's what I would say to anyone looking to pivot their career: Start doing entrepreneurial things before you transition. Start investing, networking, and building.
>
> I used Mike's forms and templates to land my first clients. One awesome result: I wrote a twelve-page ebook and priced it at $10. The book led to new coaching clients. The total return from the exercise: nearly $5,000. And it's still selling!

You can see that these stories don't need to be overly complicated. I'm not telling Matt's life story; I'm just framing the story around his inciting incident and showing how I can help the reader. The short testimonial about earning money quickly was icing on the cake.

Speaking of testimonials, let's cover a better way you can get some killer testimonials to help you accumulate more customer stories.

How to Collect Killer Client Testimonials

Whether you choose to tell the customer story yourself or ask a client or customer for a testimonial, the key is to get the right kind of testimonial—one that showcases your value and the results you get for people.

All too often, a client testimonial will sound more like a character reference than something that showcases the results you help someone achieve. "Mike is a great guy! We highly recommend him!" are nice words, but they do very little for business. There are no specific results mentioned or details on how results were achieved.

While your clients mean well, it's also likely that most are:

1. Too busy to give deep thought to writing a testimonial or
2. Sub-par writers.

To help collect better client testimonials, I use half-sentences that lead the client down a specific train of thought and bake in the inciting incident. This ensures the responses are based on results and keeps the client from feeling bogged down by heavy writing.

I recommend creating a simple "testimonial intake form" either online or as a PDF sent via email with the following sentences. Once your client fills in the answers, the natural flow of the sentences allows you to craft a client case study that you can post on your website or use in other marketing materials.

1. Half-sentence on your background: "I am the [title or position] of [organization or company], a company that [what your business is or does]..."

2. Half-sentence on the issue(s) leading you to work with me: "We were overloaded with ideas and needed a roadmap for where we were going..."

3. Half-sentence on reservations about hiring an outside consultant: "We didn't know what to expect and never worked with a consultant on such a critical issue..."

4. Half-sentence on thoughts about how I did things: "Mike was prompt, always professional, came through for late-night unexpected needs, etc...."

5. Half-sentence on results from the consultation: "Within a few months, we had a clear marketing strategy on how to launch our product..."

6. Half-sentence on your recommendation: "We absolutely recommend Mike to organizations that need to [your thoughts]..."

Feel free to take and tweak these for your own use. Keep in mind that even if you have a testimonial intake form, it may be difficult to secure testimonials. There are three other alternatives:

1. You can interview your client on a call and lead her through these questions to get the testimonial.

2. You can answer the questions for the client on their behalf and have them approve it.

3. You can take a comment they've mentioned about you somewhere online or via email and ask if you can use that as a testimonial.

As you craft your personal stories, I encourage you: *Do not overthink or overwrite*. We overestimate perfection and underestimate connection. Actually, the opposite is true. People are looking for connection, not perfection. Lean into the power of *your* stories, and you'll ensure your messaging doesn't become blender gray.

Remember, marketing isn't about closing a sale; it's about opening a relationship. While it's initially awkward, the more you share your stories, the more comfortable you will be with them. Get your stories written! Once you have a story or two fleshed out, it's time to share them on your platform.

CHAPTER FIVE

Platform:
Build Your Business
Like the Chinese Zodiac

In junior high and high school, many of my weekends were spent at one of the nearby shopping malls. If there's one thing you should know about New Jersey shopping malls, it's that they can be huge and have what seem like an endless amount of entry points. You can enter through any number of department stores, restaurants, retail bookstores, and of course, those really shady mall entrances that look like nothing more than an alleyway.

Regardless of where you entered the mall, once you were in, you were in. That's the picture I want you to have in mind when it comes to building your brand across what can seem like an endless number of platforms.

The reality is that in this day and age, our brands are like a shopping mall, and there are many entry points for people to encounter us. Some folks may hear of you through your podcast. Others may have heard you speak on someone else's podcast or at a conference. Still others may follow you via any number of social media channels or saw a video of you circulating online. A friend or colleague may have referred you. There is no shortage of places you can broadcast your message and share your story. Yet all of these roads should lead back to you and to your "home base."

The idea of a home base was drilled into me by leadership author (and my original online mentor) Michael Hyatt while I was a member of one of his coaching programs. He would often say: "Make sure you own your online home base!"

No matter how active or inactive we choose to be on social media, podcasts, or other platforms, it's vital we own our home base—like our own website or database of email addresses or phone numbers. This is really important because you actually own those assets. No one can take them away from you.

If you don't build your own website or email list, it's like the difference between a home you rent and a home you buy. Without owning your platform, you're in a home you rent.

For example, you may have a Facebook account that's all about you, but Facebook belongs to Mark Zuckerberg, not you. Facebook is a rental—and rented by billions of people. Like the villain Thanos from the *Avengers* movies, the owners of any of these other social networks can, with the snap of a finger, delete you. Poof, you're gone... and your business with you.

While we've talked quite a bit about your passions, dreams, and stories, I must remind you that you are also building a business—and any good business needs a database of prospects and customers. Even your local pizza shop has a list of addresses, phone numbers, and emails. When they need to drum up sales, they can easily email out a few coupons or mail a few flyers to prospects or past customers. Because they own that information, they can contact customers directly. If your local pizza shop has a database, you certainly need one as well.

Every Entry Point Takes You into the Mall

Let's go back to your platform and start first with websites.

When I first started out, I had a very bare-bones website that I started blogging on. I quickly realized that very few (if any) people were waking up in the morning to check my homepage, as if I were some sports site or stock market ticker. No, they were reading *internal* pages on my website: blog posts I shared on social media.

The good news is that this gave me a great deal of freedom in what I featured on my homepage. For a short time, when I was focused on landing projects as a freelance copywriter, I wrote my homepage as if I were a copywriter and spoke directly to potential clients.

This was a very different audience than the people reading my blog posts, many of whom weren't able to afford my fees and were really more interested in the topics I was writing about: personal growth, personal branding, and some life updates. These people were reading my blog from links I shared on Twitter, Facebook, LinkedIn, or some other social network—and they only saw the page my article was written on. They never even looked at my homepage!

I had two different entry points for two very different people, much like someone shopping for fancy clothes who goes through the Neiman Marcus department store entrance vs. the person who enters the mall through the movie theater to just shop around.

The only other page on my website at the time was my About Me page, which contained my headshot, a short introduction to my business, and (you guessed it) my Founder Story and Business Story. This bare-bones site was enough to land me my first clients, and once I completed those projects, I crafted Customer Stories using the testimonial intake form I outlined earlier in chapter four.

I hope this relieves you of the pressure of trying to have just one message across your entire website and social media channels. Remember, it's the same mall, but there are different entry points for different types of people.

(If you're at a loss as to what to put on your homepage, how to format it, or what to say on your website, make sure to download the bonus materials and website wireframe examples at YouAreTheBrandBook.com.)

Build Your Business Like the Chinese Zodiac

It's easy to compare yourself to others who seem to be everywhere, all the time.

I want to take that burden off your shoulders because being everywhere all the time is not a realistic or even wise way to do things. Unless you have entire teams of contractors helping you (and the money to pay them), that is not going to be an attainable goal. While every person's Path is different, allow me to share mine because it may help you in the long run.

When I started my side hustle in 2013, I was so overwhelmed by all the different opportunities out there that I decided to focus on just one at a time—all with the intent of leading people to joining my email list (my home base).

There was a great Chinese restaurant I used to frequent in college called Noodle Gourmet that turned out to be an inspiration on how I chose to build my business platforms—like the years in the Chinese zodiac.

I'm no expert on the Chinese zodiac, but I do know that every year is the year of a certain animal: the year of the horse, rat, and so forth. While I'm not a believer in that kind of stuff, I did like the year-by-year approach and decided to focus on developing one key area of my business per year. Here's a breakdown of how I stacked things:

2013—The Year of the Blog
2014—The Year of the Podcast
2015—The Year of Group Coaching
2016—The Year of the Product Launch
2017—The Year of the Live Event
2018—The Year of Speaking
2019—The Year of Video
2020—The Year of Book Writing
2021—The Year of Book Launching

I share this to show you that the things I have today were built with intent over a long period of time. As I noted earlier, Gary Keller says, "Success is sequential, not simultaneous." Could I have fast-tracked a few things? Sure, but I would have been spread thin and overwhelmed. I was just patient with it.

In 2013, I started my blog as a side hustle after I stepped away from my church music director position. I missed having a creative outlet and decided to use blogging as my platform and mandated to myself, "Come hell or high water, a blog post shall publish every Monday morning!" I missed a few days, but more often than not I hit that goal all while I was working my day job.

That year, I listened to a lot of podcasts on my commutes, which seeded the idea of starting my own podcast--but I didn't start until the following year. It was too much for me. I'm glad I waited because blogging taught me invaluable lessons on creating content and helped me get comfortable with sharing my ideas in a new way.

All Growth Comes Through Discomfort

It's easy to forget that we have to develop new muscles of creativity, self-expression, and self-promotion. Anyone can write a blog post or record a podcast, but oftentimes the biggest obstacle people face is putting themselves out there. Blogging for a year helped me slowly overcome those emotional obstacles and develop my inner mindset game.

When I started my podcast in 2014, I knew much more about writing strong headlines for my episodes, putting the episodes onto my website, and promoting my content on social media. I learned all of that from blogging, but what I didn't anticipate was how difficult podcasting would be from an energy standpoint.

I mentioned earlier that much of my career was spent in front of audiences doing music or public speaking, but podcasting was a different animal because no one was in the room with me! For podcasts, I had to supply 100% of the energy when recording. When listening to my first few episodes, I was shocked at how dry and boring I sounded. I was too dependent on an audience that wasn't there!

That stretched me and helped me develop the skills to communicate in virtual mediums, and you can bet that played a big role in helping me deliver strong webinars and host virtual coaching calls, which I started to do the following year in 2015.

The Money Shift

In 2015, I experienced a "money shift"—where all the key skills I developed helped me make much more money in much less time. I was still working my day job, but I decided this year would be the year of group coaching. I promoted a program on my blog and podcast (which gained a small but loyal audience), and it was relatively easy to fill that group.

I was spending just ninety minutes a week with twelve people and pulling in about $6,000 per month. Coupled with my freelance projects and a few low-tier products on my website, I was making enough on the side to completely quit my day job.

I was now fully immersed in the Path of the Personal Brand, and every step forward allowed me to attract new people and make new connections. All this time, I did not stop blogging or podcasting.

With time, I was able to develop the skills to do those things much faster and with higher quality—and now that I didn't have a day job, I had even more time to pursue other things to grow my brand. It's fun to get better at what you do!

In 2016, I decided to finally launch my first online course. This was the first year I was working full-time in my own business, but I still did not have unlimited resources. Building a business requires more than just resources; it requires resourcefulness. I recorded promotional videos from my laptop camera while sitting at my desk—I didn't have fancy cameras, lights, or videographers. I just used what I had.

Launching an online course required me to learn a host of new things like online advertising (I used Facebook ads), creating various landing pages, writing emails that go along with a launch, finding promotional partners, and so forth.

In 2017, I started hosting business events and workshops, which were much easier to fill because people who were in my online coaching programs wanted to meet in person. I figured I would have enough work on my plate trying to run an event and didn't want the added stress of trying to fill registrations by promoting to the general public, so I started by inviting the folks who were already in my programs.

Why Didn't I Start Public Speaking Earlier?

You may wonder why I didn't start public speaking earlier in my career. The no-frills answer is that it didn't make sense when I was starting out because I would have had to sacrifice vacation days to speak at events that I probably wasn't going to get paid for.

Also, at that time, no one knew who I was, so I figured I would continue to build my brand in the margins of my time and work my way up.

In late 2017, people started seeing videos of me online (from my own events!) and thought *Hmm, maybe Mike will speak at my event. He's been podcasting for a while so he can't be terrible, and there are photos of him on a stage. Maybe he's halfway decent!* The speaking invitations started coming, and the more I shared photos or videos for events, the more events I landed.

Get Good First

I hope this encourages you to take the time to get good at your craft. It's easy for us to look at someone who is further along and assume we have to do everything all at once, immediately. Stop! Breathe! None of this happens overnight.

You have to find what works for you based on where you are or what kind of business you're trying to build. For example, if you want to be a professional speaker, then you might start with a podcast first and start pitching events instead of creating coaching programs and online courses like I did.

What I really want you to see in my journey was that the foundation of my brand grew strong because I just really focused on making one major addition to the lineup per year.

What Do I Name My Brand or Website?

A lot of folks get stuck here, so I'll be short and sweet: You should probably just use your name.

The reason is, as a personal brand, very few people are going to refer to you by some corporate moniker. No one (who has paid me) has ever denied me work because my company wasn't "Summit Think Tank Marketing" or some other bloated, corporate name. If you can get your name as a website URL, then just use that.

Also, don't sweat it if you can't get the dot com of your name. I built my business without having a dot com for years—I used MikeKim.tv (all while doing zero video at the time). Several years into business, I hired a brokerage firm to find out who owned MikeKim.com and ended up paying the equivalent of a small car to finally negotiate the purchase. Did my sales skyrocket? No. It was purely a vanity move. I just wanted the dot com, and I had already been earning six figures a year before getting it. Don't get hung up here.

The only exception is if you plan to build a brand or website domain that you intend to sell later on. (Since it would be pretty hard for you to sell the URL of your name to someone else anyway, it's easiest just to use your name.)

Consider these names: Tiger, Gaga, Oprah, Trump, Conan, Madonna, Ellen. These folks are instantly recognizable with just a few syllables. Some are so "branded," they don't even need a first or last name anymore.

Even if you grow a brand you want to sell later, consider these names: Ferragamo, Versace, Prada, Kohler, Bentley, Cartier, L'Oréal. All of these brands are named after their founders. Even Walmart and Sam's Club are derivatives of the Walton family. No one says, "Make sure to attend that personal growth seminar hosted by Robbins International." They say, "Go to Tony Robbins' event."

As you build your platform, your name will carry an overpowering set of qualities, emotions, and associations in a way that no corporate-sounding brand can. The name of your company is not going to drive business. You are. Remember, you are the brand.

If you still prefer a more corporate name, you can go one of two ways:

1. Name your brand with terminology that identifies what the business is.

A good example of this would be Prudential Life Insurance or Sal's Pizza because the name clearly states what that business does. You can add your own name onto an identifier in the brand as well, like Williams Coaching. Playing off his unique last name, Gary Vaynerchuk named his marketing company VaynerMedia. The idea is that the brand name tells you what the business is in a very straightforward, no-nonsense way.

2. Name your brand with terminology you "shape" to mean something else.

Examples of this include Apple and Amazon. Apple took a fruit and branded it into a computer company. Amazon took the name of a river and turned it into the world's biggest online retailer. Before you do this, consider how much time and money it took to reshape what people think about these two very common words. This is a lot of work, which is why I recommend you name your brand (and website) after yourself. Don't get hung up here. Name it after yourself and move on to more important things.

Writing Your Professional Bio

Bios can sneak up on us—those pesky two-to-three sentence snippets can be really hard to write. The purpose of your bio is to succinctly sum up who you are and what you do, but it often gets overlooked as a way to draw people into taking the next step to visit your platform or subscribe to something you offer.

It's alright to have a very straightforward bio, but injecting a bit of personality can help you stand out. Since bios can be a bit tough to write, feel free to take and tweak some of these. (The copywriter in me dies a little bit whenever I read a snoozer of a bio.) I use the first one here most often:

> Mike Kim believes marketing isn't about closing a sale; it's about opening a relationship. This refreshing approach has made him a sought-after speaker, online educator, and strategist for top thought leaders. Nowadays you'll find him speaking at conferences, looking for the next great place to scuba dive, and occasionally sipping a glass of single malt whisky—all while coaching, serving clients, and recording his hit podcast, the *Brand You Podcast*.

When I submit bios for guest articles on other websites or for speaking engagements, I'll use some variation of the ones below and include an invitation to subscribe to my content. I use this one quite a bit when writing for other business sites. Notice it has a very natural call to action for a free resource:

> Mike Kim ditched his comfy C-suite marketing job in pursuit of career freedom. His goal is to help you start, run, and grow a profitable and powerful personal brand business. You can start now by joining his free 3-video series, the *Brand You Bootcamp*, at MikeKim.com/start.

Attract more subscribers by providing the promise of what the reader will attain if he or she visits your site:

> Mike Kim shows content creators simple steps for increasing conversions through powerful sales copywriting. Check out his free guides and tutorials at MikeKim.com/copywriting. His tips and tactics are sure to take your sales copy to the next level.

Writing in the present tense is gimmicky, but it can give the reader a feeling of real-time engagement and immediacy:

> Right now, Mike Kim is dodging rocks and chasing sunsets while boating off the shore of Phuket, Thailand. But you can download his short ebook that shows you how to boost email open rates by 8 to 10% every single time.

Finally, adding a bit of humor often helps, especially if it's reflective of your personality and appropriate for the situation. This bio takes a playful jab at the marketing industry.

> Mike Kim is a proven marketing pro and host of the *Brand You Podcast*. If you're ready to learn how to market your coaching business without doing stuff that would embarrass your mom, download his free "Get Coaching Clients Now" ebook here.

My LinkedIn Bio, Version 1

LinkedIn may not be around by the time you read this, but feel free to apply these bios to whatever network you feel appropriate. Since LinkedIn is a professional social network, I emphasize more of my work. There are two versions I've used almost exclusively for years, and they're quite different. The first version is based on the advice of my friend and marketing consultant John Nemo, who advocates for a more straightforward, almost resume-like style:

> WHAT I DO: I help thought leaders clarify their marketing message, monetize their ideas, and create greater impact.
>
> HOW I DO IT: I do this by incorporating an array of marketing and branding strategies including copywriting, campaign strategy, product launches, storytelling, and content marketing.
>
> WHY IT WORKS: When a brand is internally aligned with its message, it makes all of its marketing and advertising clear and compelling. In turn, this positions the brand as an authority in its niche, no matter how many other competitors there are. Clarity attracts, confusion repels.
>
> WHAT OTHERS SAY: "Mike is one of the very best copywriters I know. If you need world-class copy, then you need to contact him before he's booked by someone else!" —Ray Edwards, Founder, The Copywriting Academy
>
> "Mike adds so much value. I keep coming across lines he wrote and stuff he fleshed out that makes what I create dramatically better!" —Donald Miller, CEO, StoryBrand
>
> WHO I WORK WITH: I've helped *New York Times* best-selling authors, world-renowned speakers, and hundreds of small business owners in more than 14 different industries achieve real, measurable results using my unique approaches to marketing and brand strategy.

READY TO TALK? Reach out to me directly here on LinkedIn or visit MikeKim.com. My podcast, the *Brand You Podcast*, is consistently ranked as one of the top podcasts in Apple Podcasts on the topic of personal branding and can be accessed free at MikeKim.com/show.

EXPERTISE: Personal Brand Businesses / Thought Leadership / Information Product Marketing / Direct Response Copywriting / Product Launches

My LinkedIn Bio, Version 2

This second version is more conversational in tone. It begins with a strong one-liner and quickly showcases some teaching points to demonstrate my expertise:

Marketing isn't about closing a sale; it's about opening a relationship.

We have forgotten how to connect and engage in this digital age of automation and spammy content. There are three identities to every brand: the verbal identity (copywriting), the visual identity (design), and the value identity (positioning). All three are vital in order for your coaching, speaking, or consulting business to cut through the noise and attract clients and customers.

Over the last decade, I have worked with some of the industry's highest-paid thought leadership and expert brands. This has led me to one conclusion:

People want to buy; they do not want to be sold.

That is what great content and clear messaging can do for your business. When you understand that there are really only three reasons people consume content in the first place: 1. Education, 2. Inspiration, or 3. Entertainment, then you can tailor your marketing to your audience.

My goals are simple:

1. To guide you to write, market, and persuade in a voice that is unmistakably yours
2. To take your ideas and distill them into a framework that clearly showcases your unique value
3. To provide the right toolset to create winning launch strategies and brand awareness

For your speaking, coaching, or consulting engagements, let's connect here:

*   1:1—MikeKim.com/contact
*   Speaking—MikeKim.com/speaking
*   Or contact me via InMail

Make sure to check out my podcast interviews and testimonials in the media section below.

Connection Creator: The "Things You Didn't Know About Me" Post

Whatever channel you use to promote your business, it's important to remember that people only see you in the moment they first meet you. You may have posted on a social network for years, but if I find your profile for the first time, all I will see is your bio and last few posts.

One way to mitigate that: the "things you didn't know about me" post—a surprising way to create connection with newcomers and build deeper rapport with your current audience.

I'll often post something like this to connect with an influx of new followers, which often happens after a big speaking engagement or guest appearance on a podcast or virtual summit.

The questions are subject to change, but you can start with the following list. (Just make sure not to post really sensitive information like your birthday—identity thieves abound.)

1. Favorite food
2. Nickname as a kid
3. First job
4. Best travel story
5. Family tradition
6. What you wanted to be as a kid
7. Something you are "super particular" about

The point is to have fun with this kind of post. I'll often pull from the answers to these questions or add other things like my personality test type, favorite movie, or a band I want to see in concert. Here is an example I've used on Instagram, which is more of a lighthearted platform:

Hey, I'm Mike, and there are several of you that I've connected with recently but haven't met yet.

I'm uncle to the two cutest boys (5 and 3), a big-time NY Yankees fan (I loved them when they sucked and their cleanup hitter was Steve Balboni, so don't hate), Philadelphia Eagles, and San Antonio Spurs fan.

My hobbies include trying good scotch, scuba diving, and golf (if I can find any friends to play with).

For the past 7 years, I've worked from home as a podcaster, blogger, marketing consultant, speaker, and copywriter-to-the-stars.

I relocated for a while to West Palm Beach, FL, and I feel like I moved there 25 years too early because my neighbors had grandkids my age. But hey, the weather rocks.

On the Enneagram, I'm an 8w9, and discovering that has helped me understand life so much better.

The most valuable thing I've learned in the last year is that life isn't beautiful because it's perfect; it's beautiful because it's not.

It's nice to meet you, and I hope you have a great week. Please say hi.

Several months later, I added a few other tidbits because my current audience already saw the previous post:

Hey, I'm Mike. Been awhile since I've introduced myself so let's make this fun.

Enneagram: 8

Birthplace: California

Band I want to see in concert at Glastonbury in the evening rain with the galpal: Coldplay, Muse, U2, or just get me to Glastonbury, I'll go alone.

Last meal before death: Korean BBQ, hands down. Best I ever had was my grandmother's.

How I make my living: Teach people it's okay to pursue their dream career as a coach or creator, then teach them how to market and what to say (I *love* it).

How I left corporate: Company party on the last Friday of summer—drank beer, wine, soju, and 22 shots of Jame-O (seriously), went to the bowling alley and beat all my coworkers while lit, and said "have a nice life"—that was my last day at work.

Fave book: *Three Kingdoms*

Fave actor: DeNiro, the boss

Best meal ever: Italian Michelin chef in Phuket, Thailand, at a 5-star resort overlooking the Andaman Sea—I ate alone and it was $350, but that meal healed my soul for a night during a horrible time in life. I didn't know food could do that, and I've been looking for the same experience since.

Sports teams: Yankees, Eagles, Spurs

Most beautiful place I've ever been: Road to Hana in Maui, Hawaii—I'd go back tonight, alone if need be.

What I *truly* believe: Life is short but the longest thing we ever do—eat great food, spend time with loved ones, never pass up an adventure.

I am truly amazed at the results from these kinds of posts. Many of my clients who rarely get much engagement on social media see soaring responses from these posts.

My challenge to you: Take and tweak these examples and hit publish.

I know you want to get this right and get it perfect, but the more important thing is for you to gain the reps, build the muscle of self-expression, and put yourself out into the world in new ways.

CHAPTER SIX

Positioning:
Always Know Who
Your Competitors Are

A few years back, I took a photo from a Louis Vuitton ad for some expensive sunglasses, a handbag, and a watch and overlaid it with text from a Walmart ad. I put the doctored image into the slide deck for one of my signature speeches to illustrate a point about branding. It always gets a laugh because it's so jarring to see high-end fashion items with "Price Matching. Coupons Accepted. LOW PRICES EVERYDAY!" sprawled across the bottom.

Even a non-marketer can tell something is "off" about the image—it just feels weird. That feeling stems from a misalignment between the three sub-identities of every brand, and it is important to understand how they play off each other.

The three sub-identities of your brand are:

1.   Visual Identity
2.   Verbal Identity
3.   Value Identity

Each of these sub-identities are like legs on a stool. If one is "off," then your entire brand will be unstable. If they're aligned, then you have a clear and cohesive brand identity.

The visual identity is what most people think of when it comes to "branding" because those elements are so easy to identify. The retail giant Target literally uses a target as a logo with red as its primary color. Starbucks uses a lot of green and brown, and though you might not be able to recall their iconic mermaid in every little detail, you would certainly know her when you see her. You probably don't need as strong of a visual logo as Target or Starbucks, but your photos, fonts, and colors on your website, and even your wardrobe will play a part in your visual identity.

Your verbal identity is determined by copy: *the written content you use for any and all marketing.* Advertising, as described by famous copywriter John E. Kennedy (no, not the late President; he was John F. Kennedy) is "salesmanship in print." Your verbal identity and voice can sound academic, professional, inspirational, snarky, or use a ton of profanity (think Gary Vaynerchuk); it's up to you. You just have to be consistent with it in the same way you would be consistent with elements in your visual identity.

Your value identity has to do with positioning. Positioning is all about where you sit relative to your competitors and how the public perceives your worth. Again, Louis Vuitton is a high-end, luxury brand, and I'm pretty sure the words "discount" or "coupon" are banned from their marketing. Likewise, there is nothing luxurious or exclusive about any of the products at Walmart. The two companies have completely different value identities. Both companies make a lot of money, but they do so in very different ways because of how they are positioned in their relative markets.

A Lesson from London

Not too long ago, I went to London for the first time and got to meet one of the designers for a major fashion brand. As she was showing me around, she told me something about brand positioning that I've never forgotten.

While her company was known for selling high-end hand-bags, overcoats, and their distinctly checkered cashmere scarves, their top money maker was a lower-cost bag that was just a third of their normal prices. Yet the reason the lower-cost bag sold so well was because of the higher-end positioning of their brand. Customers were able to "buy" the status that comes with that designer's bags without breaking the bank.

When most of us start out in this space, we assume the best thing to do is to deliver high-value work for high-ticket clients—all the time. There's nothing wrong with this approach, but you can quickly end up in a feast-or-famine type situation where you're doing so much work for one client that you can't scale your time and income.

The key is to position yourself as a high-value expert and have high-value pricing but to also leverage your value to create more affordable products at scale.

Over the past several years, I've seen several of my colleagues who charge top dollar for private coaching programs follow this exact model by creating (of all things) physical day planners or journals. Michael Hyatt's *Full Focus Planner*, John Lee Dumas' *Freedom Journal*, and Tony Grebmeier's *Be Fulfilled Journal* are all great examples. For some experts, the lower-tier product has become their biggest moneymaker. However, this is only possible because they positioned themselves as a top-tier brand to begin with.

I use the Louis Vuitton/Walmart doctored image to talk about the difference between brands and how their positions are so different in the marketplace. However, there is a caveat to this comparison: Louis Vuitton and Walmart are not direct competitors. They aren't in the same industry. One is a luxury fashion brand, the other a mass-market retailer. This leads me to my first point about positioning.

1. Make Sure You Are Comparing Yourself to the Right Competitors

I'll never forget this example as it was a real wake-up call for me. I was sitting at a breakfast with some accomplished businessmen. We were going around the room sharing about our business wins and challenges. The gentleman next to me was the owner of one of the largest commercial moving companies in Connecticut.

I asked him, "Steve, how's business going?"

He said, "Mike, it's challenging. It's tough when you're in a business and your competition is basically anyone with a car. *You must always know who your competitors are.*"

I was taken aback but then realized he was right. If you're moving and have a bunch of friends who can load up some stuff into their cars or trucks, you won't hire movers!

We all have competition. This is a fact. There are countless options for prospects to give their time, energy, and money to. I say this not to discourage you but to give you a clear perspective on the reality of the situation. Yes, it's a jungle out there, but if you have clarity on who you serve and who your actual competitors are, you will be fine.

In reality, it's likely that most of the well-known voices you follow are not actually your direct competitors at all. When I first started out, the prospect of competing with the people I learned from was very daunting until I realized that I don't actually compete with most of them.

I'm quite a visual learner, so I drew a little chart to see where I fit in the landscape of marketing experts out there, which I'll show you in a moment. For now, understand that positioning is all about where you are and where your business stands against your known competition.

Determine Who You Are NOT

Positioning is a lot like jujitsu, "the gentle art." The premise of jujitsu is to leverage your opponent's size, strength, and speed against him. This allows much smaller and weaker opponents to prevail against much bigger and stronger ones.

You're not Apple, Nike, or Amazon—and your clients probably don't want you to be! They want the personal touch, someone who is relatable and approachable.

One of the ways to position yourself is to use the size of the big competitors against them by telling your clients you are *not* them. I've always found it interesting that the bigger a service gets, the smaller and more personalized the customer wants it. On the flip side for us personal brands, the smaller we are, the bigger we want to get! Like a fighter using jujitsu, it's time we used our "smallness" to gain leverage and carve out a distinct place for ourselves in the market.

This graph really helped me see where I fit in my market:

To use me as an example, I put "strategy" on one side and "tactics" on the other. Many people use those words interchangeably, so I created my own differentiation in my mind. Strategy meant that I would teach people broad concepts and philosophies and help them understand how to deploy their time, money, and resources when it came to marketing.

I considered tactics to be more "on the ground" information, like what colors work best on websites, what text works best in advertisements, and "hacks" that help you get an edge in marketing based on data.

Then, on the other axis, I mapped out the two markets: marketers vs. non-marketers. By this I simply meant that marketers were people who did marketing for a living. Non-marketers were professionals in their own right (coaches, speakers, consultants, and so forth), but they didn't earn their money as marketers.

I can't tell you how much of a relief this simple graph was to me! It was clear that I was best situated to help non-marketers build a strategy to win in their space.

Then, I used the other quadrants to map out some of the other brands I knew—and I quickly realized (to my relief) that many of the people I followed were *not* my competition!

Brands like Copyblogger, a large marketing training website, specialized in tactics and not in strategy. Folks like the brilliant Neil Patel and his company QuickSprout were really in the business of teaching professional marketers the latest SEO and traffic tactics. It requires a big team (and lots of data) to do what Neil and QuickSprout do. While I followed his work, my clients and audience weren't coming to me for more of the same.

I certainly did not fall into the category of teaching strategy to marketing professionals—this was left to global advertising agencies and big data firms that feed information to those agencies of best strategies for global marketing or political campaigns.

I had to ask myself, "What can I *not* give my clients and audience that these other brands can?" The answers were clear:

1. I could not write 2,000-word blog posts several times a week, like Copyblogger.
2. I could not create seemingly endless reports and ebooks per month, like Social Media Examiner.
3. I could not provide a website admin platform, like HubSpot.
4. I could not provide brand strategies for $1B+ entities, who normally hire firms or global agencies.

It's okay! That's not who I set out to be in the first place. This was of great relief to me.

Now it's time for you to create your own "positioning graph." If you're not sure what kind of values you should use for the X and Y axis on your graph, try these pairs:

1.   Starters vs. Experienced
2.   Nonprofessionals vs. Professionals
3.   Strategy vs. Tactics
4.   Techie vs. Non-Techie
5.   Big Spenders vs. Bargain Basement Shoppers
6.   Personal Touch vs. Corporate Feel

The value in the exercise is in seeing which "quadrant" you fall into relative to your competitors. That will give you clarity and also show you which competitors you are *directly* competing with (the ones in your quadrant) as a personal brand.

2. Once You Determine Where You Sit in the Market, Use Your Point of View and Personal Stories to Differentiate Yourself

Once I found my cozy little corner of the marketing world, I had to look around and see what other people in my market were doing and see if there was a way to further differentiate myself.

If you've worked through the personal stories I shared earlier, this won't be too difficult. Your personal stories will be first and foremost in making you stand out. Even if there is a competitor who teaches on the same subject matter and targets the same audience as you, there is differentiation because of *who you are*. The more I shared *my* point of view and personal stories, the more I stood out in my own unique way.

When I did this exercise, I realized that many of the experts I followed online weren't actually doing one-to-one coaching or freelancing work like I was at the time. They were influencers: people who created a lot of content, attracted large followings, and sold digital products.

I was an expert who worked one-to-one with clients as a coach, copywriter, or consultant, who just happened to blog. I still created content like those online influencers, but the difference was that people knew I was available for hire. I was able to provide customized, strategic insights to clients and made sure I publicized it.

As my following grew over the years, I made the transition from client and project work to creating courses and products, but this was only possible because I didn't fall into the trap of comparing myself to everyone out there. I knew where I stood in the vast landscape of marketing and seized the opportunity to use my "smallness" as a competitive advantage, all while slowly sharing my point of view and personal stories in the market.

3. Never Lower Your Positioning

When I started my first few coaching programs and workshops, I was very cognizant of positioning myself as someone who was higher tier. This was why I asked for the title of Chief Marketing Officer when I worked for the after-school academy just outside New York City—I figured that title would hold more weight than something like "Marketing Director." It paid off when I went into business for myself all those years later. No matter how you consumed my content, whether you read my blog, listened to my podcast, attended a workshop, or hired me directly, you would get the insight of a "C-suite expert."

Once I could prove to myself that I could blog regularly for several months (remember 2013 was "the year of the blog" for me), I eventually invested in hiring my friend Jason Clement to design my website to help establish my visual identity. Jason gave my site a clean, sleek, minimalist look that reflected my personality. I'm a direct, "get to the point," New Jersey kind of guy, and that is the approach I take to working with clients and teaching content.

I hosted my workshops at nice venues in attractive cities: sleek and modern business hotels in New York and Washington, DC, upscale classic hotels like the Ritz Carlton in Miami and the Driskill in Austin, and vibey workspaces in Nashville and San Diego. I wanted people to do more than simply attend a workshop—I wanted them to associate a city with me. I can't tell you how many times an attendee has said to other people during side conversations, "Oh, I love Austin. The first time I went there was for a Mike Kim event!" That is really valuable because it keeps me top of mind in their conversations for months or even years after the event.

You might assume that all this means that every piece of content I create is "upscale" and fancy, but far from it. One of the other things I consider a part of my brand is my approachability—I've heard that from many of my podcast listeners and clients.

That means that on social media, I will occasionally post things that make me relatable as a brand: pictures of my cute nephews, or self-deprecating humor, or very personal posts that have little to do with business. But I'm always careful not to overdo it. There's no exact science to this, but I would generally say that only 20% of my posts are of a more personal nature, and 80% have to do with business or branding. That's just the rhythm that works for me.

Repositioning Yourself in a New Market

I have many friends who serve as marketing directors or consultants to top personal brands. A few years ago, one of my friends was working with a blogger in the "mom" space. She had grown a huge audience of mothers who came to her for tips on cutting costs and making the most of what little discretionary time or income they had.

Here's the "problem": His client (the mom blogger) became very wealthy from her blog! She wanted to enjoy her success by buying a few high-end designer bags, going on nice vacations, and upgrading her car and home—but it felt "off-brand" to showcase all of this to her audience.

When he told me about the issue, I laughed and said, "That's a great problem to have—millions of followers and big money rolling in!"

But in all seriousness, I totally understood his predicament. (This is why positioning is so important to understand.) I suggested that he help her slowly position herself as a "business growth expert" where she could talk more freely about her journey to success. Another additional option would be to "dilute" her on her current platform by introducing new faces and voices on the blog and build a more team approach to the content that was being created.

Essentially this strategy was to create a new market (business coaching) rather than trying to reposition her in her current market. She needed to leverage her expertise as an entrepreneur to teach other entrepreneurs who would also pay more money for her insights and coaching.

"What If I Want to Do Discounts, Flash Sales, or Other Promotions?"

The short answer here: *Give a legitimate reason that does not dilute your positioning.* The best marketing strategy is to simply tell the truth. A few things I've done over the years:

1.   Run special promotions on my birthday. I will usually write about the things I've learned about business and life in the past year and tie that to a special promotional rate of one of my products or courses.

2.   When people were locked down in 2020, I ran a special discount on two of my courses and also offered live virtual coaching to accompany the course since people were stuck at home. I wanted to help people, but an unexpected thing happened—sales went through the roof, and I was able to build more rapport with my customers--all during a difficult time.

3.   I do special discounts twice a year and donate the proceeds to a charity I support. This usually takes place during Christmas and the week of my birthday. Because my birthday is six months before Christmas, the timing works out really well and, while this isn't the reason for doing so, it brings a lot of connection and humanity to my brand because my audience knows the money is going to a good cause.

Some people have strong opinions about discounts and special pricing. This is your business, and those decisions are ultimately up to you. I just don't want you to do anything that compromises your positioning. If you offer services, and those fees are not publicly known, making the decision to take on a project for less-than-ideal money is not going to publicly hurt your positioning because no one will know what you were paid.

Sometimes it is wise to make a play that allows you to work with a certain client who will actually elevate your positioning, even if you aren't paid as much as you would like. Those kinds of projects (if you're allowed to talk about them) can actually increase your positioning through association.

Every serious business understands where they sit relative to the competition. Like the owner of the moving company I mentioned earlier, you must always know who your competitors are. I challenge you to take the time to work through the graph I gave you. The clarity you gain will guide every subsequent step in the *Brand You Blueprint,* starting with the next step: Products.

CHAPTER SEVEN

Products:
Validate, Create, Refine, Relaunch

T he first time I made money online was life-changing and transformed the way I thought about money. Earlier I told you about the training company for nonprofits that I started with my friend Mary Valloni, but my part of the story goes back a few years earlier.

When I started blogging regularly in 2013, I happened to write a short article about how nonprofits could do a better job of communicating with donors and raise more support. It was written out of frustration because I had several friends who were doing missions and charitable work, and it was really difficult to donate to them because their organizations had a very poor setup.

The article spread like wildfire within my small following. Since I was getting all these views on my website, I created a small free resource to accompany that article, which readers could download in exchange for giving me their email address. Then I emailed them about a free webinar (a live online seminar) to go deeper into the topic. At the end, I offered a paid coaching program on the call.

Back then, I didn't understand brand positioning, so I just charged a small amount: $150 for four weeks of coaching for ten people. The program sold out in minutes. (I should have charged more!) Nevertheless, that $1,500 was the most life-changing money I ever made. I covered my mortgage for a month by doing a webinar.

More importantly, it was the first time I realized that it is better to be paid for my brains than my hands.

By that, I mean people were paying me for coaching and advice rather than having me actually "build" their brand by writing their copy or setting up their web pages. Additionally, the content I created for these coaching calls was repurposed later into a paid online course. I had started to take the small but important steps of moving from clients and projects to courses and products.

Now, to take some action steps and formulate your products and services, you need to start with answering two simple questions:

1.   What do you want me to pay you for?
2.   Which one of my friends would you like to talk to?

I've intentionally taken a simple, down-to-earth approach to this because it's very easy to overcomplicate the process. Remember, *business is nothing more than solving a problem for a profit*, and you should be able to answer these two questions very clearly. Let's start with the first question.

What Do You Want Me to Pay You For?

By this question, I am literally referring to what a person receives once they give you their credit card information. Is it access to you for a coaching call? A book? An online course? Something shipped in the mail? Something you write for me? A new website? An event ticket?

When I ask this question to startups, they usually answer in vague, ethereal terms like, "I want you to pay me for clarity in life" or "I want you to pay me to teach you how to attain work-life balance."

The problem is that a person cannot buy a bottle of clarity or work-life balance. That is a result, not a product. Moreover, it's a subjective result because clarity or work-life balance means something different to everyone. It's the same with concepts like significance, success, meaning, or happiness.

That's not to say you can't be in that particular line of work. The three markets of health, wealth, and relationships are broad and have many kinds of products and service providers. Right now, we need to focus on how your results are delivered, and that needs to be very clear and concrete.

When thinking through product creation, I am a very strong advocate for putting the focus on one (or more) of these three things:

1.   Time
2.   Money
3.   Skills

Your product or service should help people *gain* more time, make more money, or develop a new skill. Or vice-versa: You help people *save* time, save money, or save them from having to learn a skill (because you're doing something for them).

You may argue, "You're wrong, Mike! My coaching helps people tap into significance!" I totally understand that, but the underlying reality is that if someone has actually purchased "significance coaching" from you, they have really purchased time, money, a skill—or all three. They feel they no longer want to live a less-than-significant life and want to redeem the time they have left. Perhaps they want to make more money, making them feel more significant. Or, they purchased skills (public speaking, writing, or even being more confident on first dates or in their relationships) that make them feel more significant.

Your job is to connect your products or services to time, money, or skills because those are the most instinctive, "snail brain" reasons that people look for solutions in the first place.

If you can help people gain (or save) one of those three things, the problem you solve becomes very clear. Perhaps you help people work from home so they don't have to spend an hour commuting to work every day. Maybe you help them make more money through internet marketing or save them money by posting cash-saving hacks on your blog. You may help them gain a skill, like speaking, coaching, writing, or save them from having to learn a skill because you do those things for them.

When someone finishes one of my courses, coaching programs, or a live event, they will often say, "I gained such clarity through this experience!" but that is a by-product or result of their experience. It is absolutely the wrong message for me to use when trying to develop or market a product because those prospects have not yet experienced the transformation.

There is a huge difference between why a person buys something and what they say about it afterward. *Your front-end messaging is usually going to be different than the back-end feedback you will receive.* Most people do not know what they want or how to articulate it, but 100% of people know how to complain if they don't get it!

Your job when creating and marketing a product is to create certainty by helping them articulate what they want. There are very few things more certain than time, money, or skills.

Which One of My Friends Do You Want to Talk To?

I mentioned earlier how unhelpful "ideal client avatar" exercises can be, especially because they are based on guesswork and theory. So, instead of thinking through yet another ideal client avatar, let's reframe this as if you were asking me to introduce your product or service to one of my friends.

Which one of my friends do you want me to reach out to on your behalf? Or put another way, who would really benefit from getting to know you? Which one of my friends would really benefit from what you offer?

Would you like to talk to my friend Sara, a twenty-four-year-old grad student studying to get her pharmacy degree? Do you want to talk to my sister, who works in a consulting firm and is in her late thirties and married with two young kids under seven? Do you want to talk to my friend Henry, a single parent and corporate recruiter in his forties? Or maybe my friend Jennifer, a doctor with a daughter in college? Or my friend Wendi, an entrepreneur who runs an e-commerce company?

All of these people are vastly different, and unless you sell something that every single one of them need (like say, toilet paper!) you need to get more clarity on the person your product is geared toward.

All too often, our standards for clients or customers is "any-one who has money." It's our job as business owners to clarify the kind of client or customer we want to attract. You probably made underlying assumptions of the folks I mentioned earlier. A grad student is demographically very different from a professional who has a daughter in college—but both are very intelligent and hard-working people based on their career choices. Yet a doctor may differ psychographically from an entrepreneur entrenched in the fast-paced world of e-commerce.

One time I was asked by a freelance copywriter if I knew any-one who could use her services. I didn't know much about this person so I asked, "What kind of businesses do you help?" and the person replied, "Just anything copy-related. I can do anything."

She was making *me* do the hard work of defining *her* ideal client—even though she was the one asking me for a favor. If she told me, "I write marketing copy for information products in the business coaching space" or asked if I had any friends who were launching online courses and needed someone to write their campaigns, I would have had ten referrals for her on the spot. By saying she wrote "anything," it showed me that she didn't have clarity for herself, and as a result I didn't feel comfortable sending a referral because my name is on the line if things go sour.

In one of my coaching programs, a client posted this in our forum:

"I've been slowly working through narrowing my focus. First, I thought my focus was leaders, but that was too broad. Mike suggested I figure out, 'What results do you want to help leaders attain?'

"My mission is simple: I want to help leaders thrive and be whole for themselves, their families and friends, their teams, and their organiza-tion or business. I want them to finish well and leave a lasting legacy. In other words, I'm a coach who helps leaders across many industries (business, church, government, etc.) to thrive through coaching. Eventually I might like to add in writing and speaking, but for now I think I want this to be the year of coaching rather than try to do everything at once. Thoughts?"

My response:

"Hey [name withheld], I know this can be hard, but wrestling with this is part of the process, so I totally commend you! It would be very hard to market your business because the outcomes are still too broad. There are too many. You mentioned nine things alone in your post:

1. Thrive and be whole
2. Themselves
3. Their families
4. Their friends
5. Their teams
6. Their organization
7. Or business
8. Finish well
9. Leave a lasting legacy

"You need to pick just one. The others will follow and can be residual, but you can only be one. I hired a relationship coach for a time. Did it have a good effect on my business? Of course. My family? My team? Yes. But I clearly hired her for relationships. Any spear needs a tip, and this is still too broad. Honestly, it's not even believable that any one coach could do all of this well."

For this gentleman, getting clarity was a longer process, and that is totally okay. But can you see how catastrophic it would have been for him to create an online course that taught all nine of those things? He would have poured in hours of work and thousands of dollars in product creation and marketing only to realize no one would have purchased his program. That would have left him demoralized, and he might have possibly given up his entrepreneurial dreams forever.

The Five Plays of the Personal Brand Expert

It's no secret that the most successful coaches, speakers, and thought leaders are monetizing their expertise through information products. At some point, you may want to do the same by "productizing" what you do with clients and projects and build multiple revenue streams through online courses, products, or high-ticket events. But I'm going to be real with you right now. There is a prerequisite to productization and that is having a high-level skill in either speaking, writing, coaching, or consulting *first*.

Trying to productize right away would be like some guy thinking he could play in the NBA simply by imitating one of LeBron James' signature highlights, like his historic chase-down block against the Golden State Warriors in the 2016 Finals.

Our guy goes to his local basketball court, runs up and down the floor, leaps across the lane, and tries to soar through the sky and pin a ball against the backboard. Yet he hasn't worked on his conditioning, agility, or vertical leap. He can't shoot, rebound, dribble, or pass. He simply practices that one play and thinks it will make him a basketball great. Sounds ludicrous, right? Yet this happens *all the time* in the personal brand space.

These are the five "plays" of the personal brand expert:

1. Speaking
2. Writing
3. Coaching
4. Consulting
5. Productization

I've had the privilege of working with some of the biggest names in the thought leadership space, and I can say unequivocally that every single one of them who successfully productized did so because they mastered one or more of the first four "plays" of speaking, writing, coaching, or consulting. Only then were they able to productize.

People want to productize by creating online courses, building certification programs, or writing books, but they don't realize productization is really the last play in the playbook, reserved for those who have developed at least one of the skills that come before it. For example, Marie Kondo was a consultant and wrote a book before she sold her home goods. Brené Brown was a writer and speaker before she launched her certification program. Michael Hyatt did a considerable amount of speaking and writing before launching his online courses.

How can you productize (and sell) a course when you haven't done even one of those first four things yet? This is why there is such a glut of poor information products out there. I've fallen victim to plenty of them. I'd purchase a product because the marketing was terrific, only to look into the course and find that it was "101" level stuff they seemed to have copied and pasted from someone else.

This is why I'm going to push you to validate your offerings and develop your skills *all while you're doing it*. Think about what you will gain: tremendous amounts of experience speaking on camera, writing up teaching points, consulting in real time by answering questions, and coaching people through their challenges. All of these skills are going to be invaluable to you when you step into a studio to record an information product or sit down and write content that goes into a book.

Moreover, you truly do become like LeBron James, at least when it comes to sharing your expertise. When called upon, you can speak, whether from a stage or behind a computer screen. You can write content for presentations or your social media accounts. You can coach people one-on-one or in groups or consult clients privately. The "real time" game situation dictates which of these plays you decide to run. If you're truly up to becoming a genuine expert who creates terrific products, here's the process I recommend:

Validate, Create, Refine, Relaunch

Your first goal when creating a product is to get proof of concept. Hear this carefully: You cannot simply manufacture something and then market it, *hoping* it will sell.

Look at the marketing campaigns for any huge blockbuster movie coming out and you'll see they market the movie well before it's even finished. But during that time, they are continually pulling together small focus groups to give the creators feedback on the product. Then they go on to the big launch.

Here's the four-step process I follow when creating more robust offerings. (I often do this for free because the feedback is worth it.)

1. Validate the key problem and identify the top result that prospects want.

2. Create a beta group and solve the problem with your prospects. This will naturally require you to coach, consult, speak, or write.

3. Refine the program and see if there is a better vehicle by which to solve the problem, whether it is an online course, workshop, book, or coaching. (You will be able to set up different income streams this way.)

4. Relaunch the program and sell it in the new medium as a course, book, workshop, or some other product.

If you shortcut any of these steps, you will miss out on key insights that can mean all the difference between the success and failure of your offer.

The first thing I do when validating an idea is to identify the key problem. Here's an email I sent out to colleagues and friends individually when I first got started—before I had a big database of readers.

> SUBJECT LINE: This may not be for you, but…
>
> Hey [name],
>
> I'm putting together a training about [topic] and thought you might be interested!
>
> Can I pass some info along to you?

Warning: Do not write anything after the question at the end of the email. Do not say thank you. Do not say, "I hope you're well!" You must end the message with a question. This creates an open loop that is almost too difficult to ignore.

What happens if a person replies with a yes?

Send them this next email. You may not even need a new subject line. Just reply to their email in the same thread. If you start a new email, just use the subject line below:

> SUBJECT: Two quick questions!
>
> Hi [name],
>
> Awesome! Really quick, I have two questions:
>
> 1. What's your biggest question about [topic]?
>
> 2. What blogs, books, or podcasts do you go to in order to learn more about [topic]?
>
> Would you let me know?

If you think this is simple, it is. Simple things work. Start with ten people. It's likely you'll get at least one or two positive responses. If it worked once, then it can work again. Pick ten more people. Do the work.

Why send the second email? Because I'm teaching you to make a habit of gathering data. *Professionals use data to make marketing decisions.* The reason you should ask what books, podcasts, or blogs they turn to is because you want to understand who your competitors are. You must send that second email if they respond with a yes to the first. Do not deviate from the plan.

At this point, it is up to you to decide how you want to stay in touch with the folks who have said yes. An easy way to do it is to invite your list to a private online forum. I used a program called Basecamp early on, and these days I use a communication platform called Slack.

You cannot build your business while sitting in a luxury box at the ballpark. You may be able to impress people from a distance, but you can only impact them from up close. Get on the field and grind in the dirt with your people.

Once you help these folks, you can ask for testimonials, hone your content, and relaunch the training with paid members.

Taking the time now to follow this process will ensure that you create a product or service that truly helps people. In return, people will give you their hard-earned dollars and spread the word about what you have done for them.

This is exactly how I created the *Brand You Blueprint*. It took many iterations, and I continually honed the approach based on the work I did with real clients over the years. My clients were able to show me where they were getting stuck in the process, but when things worked, I was also able to help anchor them in their wins.

Only after these many iterations could I, in good conscience, put my process into the book you're reading now and share it with a much wider audience.

Where Do You Want the Money to Come From?

Now that we've covered the pathway to products, let's get an overview of the income streams you want to create. Divide a sheet of paper into three columns. On the left column write "services," in the middle column write "hybrid," and on the right side write "products." Services will fall into the active income category, meaning you'll be trading time for dollars. Passive income will be revenue you generate through products you create once and sell on an ongoing basis afterward. Hybrid income is a bit of both, such as an online course that you supplement with, say, monthly coaching calls for a year.

Now list anything and everything that will pay you money that you have in your business or want to have. A sample may be something like this:

INCOME STREAMS

SERVICES (ACTIVE INCOME)	HYBRID	PRODUCTS (PASSIVE INCOME)
COACHING (1:1 OR GROUP)	COURSE + COACHING	AFFILIATE INCOME
CONSULTING PROJECTS	COACHING + COURSE	DOCUMENTS & TEMPLATE FILES
FREELANCING		COURSES
LIVE EVENTS		BOOKS
PUBLIC SPEAKING		

Here's the general rule for the things I listed above: *Lower price requires higher traffic.*

For example, it's wonderful to create a course or write a book, but if you want to make money, you will need to garner a lot of web traffic and leads because those products are cheaper. You'd have to sell a lot of books to make six figures in income.

This is why I started out as a coach, consultant, and freelance writer. Not only did it allow me to develop those valuable skills, I simply didn't have a large enough audience to sell passive, lower-tier products to at the time.

We've covered the Validate, Create, Refine, Relaunch process, so now let's turn our attention to a few products you can create. I'll cover two here, Affiliate Commissions and Documents & Templates.

Affiliate Commissions

This one is easy because it doesn't take much time to set up. The payoff won't be huge at the start because you may not have a large audience to sell to, but the income from this will grow as your audience grows.

Consider what tools and apps you're using and see if you can sign up to be an affiliate with any of these products or services. One of my earliest affiliate products was for a web hosting company I used. I recorded a screencast on how to set up a hosting account with them and shared it with my audience. I earned a $65 commission per signup recommending this on my fledgling blog, all while I was still working my full-time day job. I kept thinking, "Sixty-five dollars is more than most people make an hour!"

I found out that the email service provider I used for marketing also had an affiliate program, as did the software I used for capturing email addresses. My podcast producer had an affiliate program, as did a productivity app that I used to keep track of my to-do list. Over the years my "tech stack" has changed, but whenever I do change my tools, I always look to see if they have an affiliate program. (If you want a current list of tools I use to run my business, go to MikeKim.com/tools.)

The beauty of affiliate income is that it scales. You create it once, new people keep signing on, and it helps accelerate your income.

A quick note here before we move on. Recommending other people's tools, products, and resources is wonderful, but I encourage you to only endorse products that are congruent with your brand. Don't do it just to make money; that doesn't work well. Your audience will be able to tell, and they will lose their trust in you. Your name is ultimately on the line, so be picky about who you promote. When I recommend any kind of product, it's my personal policy that it be something I truly enjoy, find helpful, and believe in.

Documents & Template Files

Selling documents and templates is another easy way to break into selling passive income products. They don't take a lot of time to create and don't require a big marketing campaign to promote.

Since most of my audience is composed of entrepreneurs or aspiring entrepreneurs, I simply create forms, templates, and documents I wish I had when starting out, even if they aren't related to marketing, such as:

1. Client Proposal Templates
2. Sales Call Scripts
3. Workflows and Standard Operating Procedures

No, these aren't "sexy" products, and it's not likely I could create an entire full-time living based on them, but they have brought in a considerable amount of income over the years because my audience has grown.

Taking your day-to-day processes and selling them is what I call the Tater Tot Principle. Tater tots were invented in 1953 when American food company Ore-Ida founders F. Nephi Grigg and Golden Grigg were trying to figure out what to do with the leftover tips of cut-up potatoes after making French fries. They took the leftover bits, added some flour and seasoning, and turned them into a frozen food empire!

I applied this principle to a recent product consisting of workflow templates created by my Director of Operations, Chelsea Brinkley. Chelsea has worked with me since nearly the start of my business, and over the years, she has created workflows for nearly all our processes: podcast creation, social media content creation, live event booking, travel booking, coaching and consulting contracts, and more.

We recorded a series of podcast episodes on how we work together and created these workflows, and they've gone on to be a really nice revenue stream for the business.

Stop Letting People Pick Your Brain for Free

I can't close this chapter talking to you about providing services without encouraging you to set up healthy boundaries for yourself. Call me crazy, but I don't think anyone should be able to buy a block of your time or "pick your brain" (especially for free) without you having a say.

I always have a process if someone wants to work with me one-on-one or in a smaller group coaching or mastermind program. A simple application or intake form will often give you most of the answers you need to decide whether you want this person as a client or not. (Telling brain-pickers I have a one-on-one coaching option is also a great way to protect my time and energy. If they want free advice, they can listen to my podcast or read my blog.)

If someone wants to work with me, the process is simple:

1. They fill out a client intake form or application. (I then decide whether I want to move forward with them or not.)
2. If I feel good about it, I send them a link to book a call.
3. We talk and then take the next steps on them working with me one-on-one or joining one of my groups.

You may think, "Mike, this sounds good in theory, but do you seriously make *everyone* fill out your form?"

Well, yes. Even big-name clients have filled out my form. This reinforces my positioning, and I can often tell how serious someone is about working with me if they can't even oblige a simple request to fill out a form or use a call scheduler.

I have pushed off well-known names in my industry simply because they didn't want to respect my process and how I manage my time and business. I can only imagine what kind of boundaries those folks would cross if I ended up working with them.

Having an actual personal brand business positions me as a partner, collaborator, and sometimes as a mentor to my clients, even if they are much bigger than me. While everyone else is pining to work with these kinds of people as a freelancer, I am positioned much higher.

This is why everything I've had you do up to this point matters. You have a point of view, personal stories, a platform, and you are clear on your positioning. As your brand grows, you decide who you work with, not the other way around.

I challenge you not to shortcut the process. Validate, create, refine, and relaunch. If you do this with intention, you will create your own framework, process, or methodology that will position you as a true thought leader rather than the many thought repeaters that are out there.

In the next chapter, you'll learn some practical ways to help you determine your pricing and set your fees for standalone projects, as well as some real-world examples on how to raise your prices with current clients.

CHAPTER EIGHT

Pricing:
People Like to Buy,
They Do Not Like to Be Sold

For most people, the recipe for pricing sounds like some exotic cocktail with equal parts of psychology, strategy, and time stirred together with a sprinkle of math. The good news is that if you are clear on your positioning and the kind of product you are offering, the price becomes a little bit easier to determine.

Let's start with hourly rates. I'm generally not a big fan of charging by the hour because as a whole, hourly pricing creates a conflict of interest. Your client is trying to spend as little money as possible, and you are trying to make as much money as possible. Worse, the project ends up being measured on time, which places a focus on input rather than output. If I hire a web designer, I don't really care how many hours she has spent on the project. I don't want a line item on the receipt for "hours of labor" like I would get from a car mechanic. I just want a good website and to be charged fairly. There are honest mechanics out there, but I'm pretty sure some of the ones I've used have taken their sweet time to run up the bill.

In some industries, charging by the hour makes sense—like getting a spa treatment, massage, or working out with a physical trainer. Other industries historically charge by the hour, but in truth, they are frustrated they can't change their industry. Ask any attorney if he or she likes hourly billing and chances are they hate it because the better they get, the quicker they can do the work—yet the less money they make. Unfortunately, that's just how their industry works. We'll address how to move away from hourly billing later in this chapter, but for now, let's talk about how to charge hourly.

What Is Your "Traffic from Hell" Hourly Price?

There is a simple guideline I've used to determine hourly rates I call the "Traffic from Hell Principle" (and remember, I'm from New Jersey). Let's say I have cash to give you. The only catch is that you have to drive through an hour of the worst traffic you can think of to claim it. I can literally feel the angst bubbling up thinking about the countless days of gridlock I've spent going in and out of New York City. The George Washington Bridge, Lincoln Tunnel, Holland Tunnel isn't just the path from New Jersey into the Big Apple; they are where hopes and dreams go to die.

Anyway, go ahead and name a place you've been with horrendous traffic—New York City, Los Angeles, Atlanta, or even your local town on a Friday night at 5 p.m. If you had to sit through thirty minutes of bumper-to-bumper, standstill, not-going-anywhere traffic to pick up cash and then drive back home for another thirty minutes, how much would I have to give you? $50? $100? $500? $1,000?

This principle has always helped me determine hourly rates. Currently, the only thing I offer at an hourly rate is a one-on-one coaching call, which someone can sign up for through my "fill out the form, book a call, we'll talk" process I outlined earlier. When I first offered this call, I charged $100. Then I charged $300, then $500. At one point, I charged $1,297 for the one-hour call, and people signed up for it.

You may be incredulous at the idea of paying that much to talk to someone for an hour, but these folks did not. It probably means you do not think there would be that much value in the call, but value is subjective. They got value because it wasn't about the time—it was about the *solution to their problem.*

As my business kept growing, my time became more and more valuable to me. Even the $1,297 per hour for an individual consult wasn't something that made sense when I looked at what I was earning by spending an hour on a coaching call with multiple people or a webinar that brought in more buyers.

You might ask, "Mike, would you drive thirty minutes and back for $5,000 cash?" Perhaps.

But I surely don't want to take a $5,000 copywriting contract that will take me thirty hours to finish when I can sell a workshop ticket for $5,000 per person with multiple attendees.

Please understand that I am not sharing this to boast. I want your business to grow to whatever size, proportion, or value that you want, and that is exactly my point. You have the right to determine how you run your business, and if it works for you, then I am happy to cheer you on. But my advice is to always be careful about trading too much time for too little money.

Pricing Tiers for Products

When it comes to pricing products, like online courses, books, or other information products, most people simply go by what they think the market will bear. Rather than just copy what others are charging, let's think through this in a more intentional way by setting up some pricing tiers.

I often consider the lowest tier of pricing to be anything **under $100**, and these will usually be straight-up passive income products that do not include any kind of support in terms of live calls or ongoing coaching. When it comes to my own information products, I will often charge at increments of $29, $49, or $97. There isn't necessarily any magic to these numbers—I've just found them to work well for me. Anything under $100 usually falls under the "impulse buy" category, meaning that people don't really need to think too much about the purchase.

The second tier of products is between **$100 and $500**. You will often see people price these products at increments of $197, $297, $397, and $497 or swap out the last number and just charge $199, $299, $399, or $499. I may supplement products in this tier with some coaching calls occasionally, but it's very possible to sell passive products at these prices with no ongoing support.

(As soon as you get over $500, data seems to show that you've moved past the threshold of an impulse purchase. People seem to think more about purchasing anything over that amount, so this is just something to be aware of.)

The third tier of products gets into the higher figures: **$500–$1,999**. I've seen price points of $797, $997, $1,297, $1,497, and $1,997. Obviously, these are more robust programs that are often hybrid products, meaning the buyer receives access to an online course but also gets a live event ticket or ongoing coaching calls. You will often see payment plans offered in this tier.

The fourth tier is really anything that is **above the $2,000** price point. Products or services in this range may require a sales call or require the services of a sales rep. Prospects will often want to talk through the purchase to make sure it is right for them. One of my past clients sold a certification program for use of his intellectual property for anywhere between $5,000 and $7,500 and had an entire full-time sales team because of the financial commitment involved.

These tiers are not hard-and-fast rules, and you do not need to have an offer in every single one of these tiers. They are meant to serve as guidelines to help you sift through some of the confusion. If you have positioned a product to hit a higher type of buyer and deliver big value, you should price accordingly.

On the flip side, it is important to realize that just because a product is cheaper does not necessarily mean that it is easier to market. Remember that the lower the price of a product, the higher amount of traffic you need—and in that regard, you will still need to write copy, build web pages, and create marketing collateral for your product regardless of the price.

The Psychology of Pricing

There is a story about a beach town souvenir shop owner who had some turquoise jewelry she couldn't sell. No matter what she tried, no one was purchasing the jewelry. One weekend, she went away for a vacation and wrote a note to her weekend manager, "Mark 1/2 off," but being that her handwriting was a bit sloppy, her manager thought she wrote, "Mark 2X"—doubling the price of the jewelry. When the owner came back to the store, she found out that all of the jewelry sold out at double the price! Pricing often reflects value.

Another principle that has really helped me understand the psychology of pricing is the "Cupcake and Cookie" split test. A split test (or A/B test) involves making two different versions of an offer and simply seeing which one works better. There is a famous split test often cited by marketers and pricing consultants taken from a bake sale.

1.   Offer 1: $1 for a cupcake and two cookies
2.   Offer 2: $1 for a cupcake, get two FREE cookies as a bonus

Offer 2 far outperformed the first offer even though the buyer gets *the exact same thing for their money!*

The principle here is that simply repositioning things in your offer can lead to dramatically different results. Offer bonuses and bundles in a way that makes your prospect feel smart.

The Bonus Sandwich

If that's true, then it begs the question: How do I know which bonuses to include in an offer?

Years ago, I heard Derek Halpern, founder of Social Triggers, talk about something he called the Bonus Sandwich, which I found extremely helpful.

1.   Top piece of bread: a highly valuable, limited bonus that may be more valuable than the offer itself

2.   The meat and veggies of the sandwich: your offer

3.   Bottom piece of bread: a bonus that is valuable and scalable, which supplements the offer

One of the things I often do when selling an online course ("the meat") is to offer a "top piece of bread" bonus of a one-on-one call to the first ten people who register for the course (I share how much I normally charge for that call, which adds the perceived value because it's my time). The bottom "piece of bread" bonus might be a suite of documents and templates that are normally sold on my site at a lower-tier price point but would still be very valuable to members of the course.

I've seen others offer bonuses like a ticket to a live workshop or several months of coaching calls. Obviously this kind of offer would fall into the "hybrid" column because there is still a lot of active time being given to fulfill those bonuses.

The point is, this is all up to you. Study other pricing models and see what you are comfortable committing to. Some people will offer a "VIP" level to a program that contains coaching calls and some bonuses and offer a "home study" level where people just get the videos and do not want to pay for the extras.

Charge What You're Worth, Then Add 20%

As you can imagine, pricing projects can feel like you're just shooting in the dark because of the uncertainties of the deal. The variables: You're not sure what the budget is for the client, you're not sure how much work the project will entail, and you're not sure if the client will be easy to work with.

Before I go into sharing some ways to price a project (thanks to some good friends of mine), let me at least propose one tip. Whatever number you decide to charge, add 20% and you will be amazed at how much better you feel. That extra 20% can give you the extra juice to push through the headaches of traveling to the client or event, power through the messy middle of a project, or put up with some of the unforeseen challenges that come your way. Get used to assigning more value to yourself than you normally would. Sadly, most people tend to undervalue themselves.

Value Pricing for Projects

There are several folks I've had the pleasure of knowing who have been of tremendous value when it comes to pricing, the first being Kirk Bowman, who I met in a peer coaching mastermind group. Kirk is the founder of a software company called Mighty-Data and host of the *Art of Value* podcast—and he was one of the first people I met who practiced value pricing.

According to Investopedia.com, value pricing is a strategy of setting prices primarily based on a consumer's *perceived value of the product or service in question.*

Value pricing is customer-focused pricing, meaning companies base their pricing on how much the customer believes a product is worth.

Kirk's first value pricing proposal was for a custom healthcare application. After identifying the value that the project would create for the customer, he doubled the price he would normally have charged and won the contract. Within twelve months, Kirk made the switch from hourly pricing to value pricing with all his clients, and his revenue increased by 56% the first year. The next year, his revenue increased by 79% and he "never looked back."

I interviewed Kirk on my podcast not long after we met, and it was one of the most insightful conversations I've ever had on value pricing. I took a copious amount of notes from our conversation, and one of the most helpful things he shared with me was his 9-Box Method of pricing for projects.

The 9-Box Method to Creating Pricing Options

I've put my own spin on Kirk's 9-Box Method based on my experience using it for my own projects and teaching it to others. The key is to create a 3x3 grid to help you visualize what you are going to charge based on the amount of value the client will get from working with you.

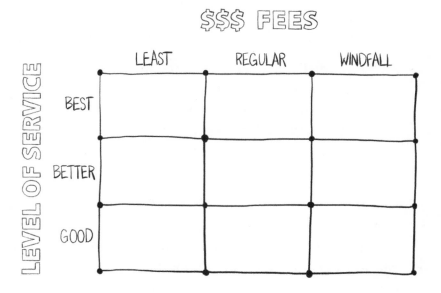

On the left side of this grid, you can set the boxes to say Good, Better, and Best to represent the level of service you will provide. (Obviously, I don't mean the quality of your work because I believe you should always provide the best work possible. I'm simply talking about how involved you are in the project and how much value the client receives.) Across the top of the grid, write down Least, Regular, and Windfall for the amount you will charge for each level of service.

» The Least amount is the lowest amount of money you would do the project for. Anything below that is not suitable.

» The Regular amount is what you feel comfortable with. Think of this as a "manufacturer's suggested retail price," which you'll often see for cars, electronics, and appliances. Like any vendor, you can change this price, but you should have a ballpark idea of your standard fee for this level of service. (Make sure to add that 20%!)

» A Windfall amount is something that you would be extremely happy with. If you don't set an outrageous windfall amount, you will never win a windfall contract. It's really important that, in your psychology, you learn to really lean into what makes you uncomfortable. Get that number out there.

(One of the benefits of using the 9-Box Method is that it will force you to evaluate and clarify what your Good, Better, and Best offers entail. Each project you consider may be different. I use a separate 9-Box grid on every single project.)

Again, when it comes to the level of service, you simply want to consider your level of involvement in the project and the value the client receives.

For example, several years ago, my good friend Dr. Michael Hudson asked me to help one of his clients, a very large financial institution, rebrand their entire organization. Michael wanted to know how much my fee would be, but being an experienced consultant himself, he knew I would present a few options based on my level of involvement and the value provided.

In this instance, Good service meant a few virtual video calls with the client's marketing team. I would look through their ideas, provide several ideas of my own, and give high-level strategic insight into their rebranding campaign. Essentially, they would drive the car and I would guide them while sitting in the backseat.

Better service meant that I would fly cross-country to their headquarters on two separate occasions for a two-day planning session with their marketing team, and at a later date, for a two-day planning session with their executive team. I would also offer virtual calls both before and after the in-person meetings and be available to them through the entire process of the rebrand up until launch. To continue with the car analogy, they would drive the car, but I would be sitting in the front seat as a navigator, telling them which turns were coming up next, when to make certain decisions, and what I saw coming ahead.

The Best level of service would include everything already offered as well as directly writing the marketing collateral for their rebrand, including commercials, online ads, and billboards, as well as internal communications to their employees. I would also fly back out to their city for their big rebrand event where their CEO would unveil the rebrand to their entire workforce (over a thousand people) gathered in an arena for a big celebration and possibly make myself available to present the rebrand ideas to the audience onstage. In this case, I would be driving the car and the client would be sitting in the front seat.

Then I set fees for each level of service. I start with "least" because I've found that it is easier for me (and most people I teach this to) to start with the minimum amount they would charge for a project. This provides a baseline to work up from. Then I fill in the rest of the boxes appropriately.

Once you draw up these numbers, you can decide which numbers you will put in the proposal: the Windfall, the Regular, or the Least.

It's also very important to present three options of working together: Good, Better, or Best. This gives the prospect choices. If you only present one option, you severely decrease your chances of landing any work. *Remember: People love to buy; they do not like to be sold.*

Using the 9-Box Method also gives you great freedom in how you price certain clients. You can, as my friend Paul Klein says, "Price the client and not the project." There's no rule that you need to charge everyone the same amount for the same amount of service. This loops back into the concept of value pricing. The stakes involved in the rebrand project for the financial client are significantly higher than, say, someone rebranding a podcast that has a very small following. The value is much different because of what is at stake for the client.

Finally, using the 9-Box Method also allows you to charge appropriately for clients who may turn out to be a headache. If you charge a demanding and high-strung client (the kind who emails and calls you at all times of the day, nonstop) you may be able to tolerate the project if you're earning a windfall amount of money. If you charged that person your "least" amount or just threw a number out there, you may end up in a situation where you're doing best-level work for the least amount you would charge for your lowest level of service.

Don't skip out on using the 9-Box Method!

How to Raise Your Prices

It is very likely that at some point in your business, you will need to raise prices. Rightfully so!

If you are getting better at what you do and are adding greater value to clients, you deserve to make more money. But how do we raise prices, whether it be to a new client or existing clients?

If you need to raise your prices for existing services to *new* clients, it is easy: Just raise the price. They don't have any pre-existing notion of what you would charge anyway, so you can simply go into the project with a new baseline.

That's precisely what I did with my first few clients. Let me explain.

I charged one of my very first clients $500 for what ended up being quite a bit of work. I spent several hours on the phone with him for a few weeks, and he needed me to write copy for his website, help him price his packages, grow his social media, and set up his email list. Crazy, I know. But he was one of my first clients, so I delivered big for him. I wanted his business and his testimonial about what I could do.

He experienced great results from our project together and was happy to refer a colleague to me who needed similar work done for his business. The only difference is that I charged this referral client $2,000. I went from client one to client two with a 300% markup.

Here's the kicker: For client two, it took me less time to do what I did for him than it did for client one. If I charged hourly, I would have *lost* money. But this is value-based pricing, which allows you to charge more for being better at what you do.

After client two, every new client set a new baseline for my fees. For my third client, I charged 20% more. That client had terrific results, and since I saw how much value I was bringing to my clients, I continued raising my fees.

As my expertise and brand have grown over the years, I now routinely charge five to six figures for private work.

A Simple Script for Raising Your Prices

Now if you are raising prices to your existing clients for a current service you provide, this can be a bit trickier. Much of the issue has to do with how you communicate the price change.

One of the best examples I've seen of this is from my long-time podcast producer and fellow mastermind member, Danny Ozment.

Danny runs Emerald City Productions, a marketing company that specializes in helping businesses create top-notch podcasts. Danny's experience as a Nashville studio owner certainly speaks volumes for the sound quality of his clients' shows (mine included), but he is also on the cutting edge of the podcast industry and produces some of the biggest shows on the market. Because there is actual time spent by Danny's team on every episode they produce (they have to listen to an episode in order to edit it) he eventually had to raise his fees.

Dear [Client],

This has been a year of tremendous growth and learning for me and my business. You were a catalyst for that growth this year, and I am so grateful to you for that!

First a quick story... Over the first half of the year, I ran ads on "She Podcasts" sharing tips about how to improve the sound quality of your podcast, and as part of that campaign, I offered free sound assessment calls to podcasters.

I averaged 7 calls per month, and I was surprised by the experiences that people shared with me.

At least half of the people I spoke with mentioned that they had previously worked with or were currently working with well-known podcast production companies. Companies that are highly visible at big conferences. We both know several of them…

Without fail the experiences I heard were the same…

1. "I felt like no one cared about my show."
2. "It seemed to me that I was working with interns…"
3. "I never got to work with the person who drew me to their service."
4. "It definitely wasn't worth the money I was paying."

Now, I could have been hearing only from hard-to-please people. I thankfully am blessed to have amazing clients like you. People who are appreciative and easy to work with…

These calls, however, hardened my resolve to provide hands-on, boutique, concierge-level service and hand-crafted quality to all of my clients, drawing on my experience as a professional recording engineer. I wanted to be able to be flexible. To be able to take care of my clients at the 11th hour. To personally oversee and sign off on every episode that moves through Emerald City Productions.

To keep that level of service and quality means that I must restrict our workload to no more than 20–25 episodes per week.

So, in order to maintain this level of quality and attention for you and all of my clients, over the past year I have grown my team by adding a project manager and several experienced full-time recording engineers as editors and mix engineers, purchased the highest level of processing and analysis software, and added more services to my currently advertised production packages.

I have also raised rates significantly for new clients.

To grow my business, I am making this additional change.

To charge commensurate to the value I bring, you will be asked to upgrade to more recent rates by March 1st because you are on a lower/older rate.

As a valued client, I'm going to give you the first opportunity to occupy positions in the production calendar.

If that doesn't work for you, I totally understand, but if you want to continue with me, here is your new rate that will go into effect by March 1st for my Standard production package: $X.

This rate is below my current advertised rate. This is a loyalty discount in honor of your time as a valued client. This rate will not change for at least two years.

The Standard package includes the services already present in your service PLUS additional services and benefits (listed below) that will be added to your current service as a result of the upgrade to the Standard package.

Please note that the services in BOLD are upgrades that are not normally available in the Standard package but have been added as a loyalty bonus for you.

New rate: $X

New parameters and added services: [List of Added Services]

Do you feel like this is something that will work for you?

If not I completely understand, and we can drop your level of service down to my Essential package in order to keep the price at $X / month. You can review the Essential package, but the major difference is that it doesn't include detailed editing in real time.

If neither of these options works for you, I will do all I can to help you find a lower-cost option that will meet your budget needs.

Thank you for being a valued client for so long.

I am very grateful that you have stayed with me so long and that we have been able to make your show sound high quality and professional. I also hope that I have given you time each week to do what you do best and grow your show, community, and business.

I hope you will choose to stay with me and allow me to continue to help you as you grow in the future.

With love and appreciation!

Danny

When Danny pitched this offer to his clients, *not a single one objected.*

One thing Danny did really well early on in his business was to position himself as a top-tier producer. He did a wonderful job of telling his Founder Story and Business Story: He is a huge believer in podcasts and found that they were the best way for him to grow personally and professionally while tending to his family. As I mentioned, he was also a former studio engineer in Nashville, the music capital of the world, and that gave him a level of authority that few others could match. Danny established his position with certainty through his stories, products, services, branding, and yes—his pricing.

Even when you raise your rates with your long-term clients, they may well pay it. People don't like change. It will be hard for people to replace you, so they will often pay the newer rates because it's such a pain to go out and find someone else to do for them what you do. Money follows impact!

It is amazing how we tend to overlook the value we provide others and then have pricing guilt when we quote clients. Don't overestimate others and underestimate yourself. Your gift is your normal. Your normal is someone else's "weird." They wonder how you can see things the way you do, solve problems the way you do, and create outcomes with just a few deft touches. Price accordingly, friend.

CHAPTER NINE

Pitch:
The Most Effective Marketing Strategy Is to Simply Tell the Truth

I told you earlier about the telemarketing job I landed while taking a semester off in college. While I didn't appreciate having to lie for a living, one thing that job taught me was the importance of following a script for sales pitches. I was also trained to "read" the prospect and evaluate how ready he or she was to buy.

In the years since, my understanding of sales pitches deepened as I studied copywriting. In this chapter, I'm going to give you the simplest frameworks and tools I use every single day to *pitch offers and make sales.* The simpler your tools, the more likely you will use them. I do not believe you need to be a highly trained sales shark in order to succeed, but you do need to have some basic understanding about how to use scripts, craft marketing campaigns, and understand a prospect's level of awareness.

Before we dive in, I want to make sure I preface all of these tips by saying that the most effective marketing strategy is to simply tell the truth. Don't lie. If (and when) you get caught, you'll do irreparable damage to your brand. Now, allow me to share a story that will help frame the rest of what we'll cover in this chapter.

A Prospect's Five Levels of Awareness

Some time ago, a young woman I'll call Nancy attended one of my workshops to work through her business idea of creating "healthy homes." I wasn't quite sure what she meant. Nancy explained that being a military family, her family moved several times over the course of a few years and noticed they would experience terrible headaches in some houses but not in others. She stumbled upon a video online about how some electric meters emit radio waves or even low-level RF radiation, which may cause headaches.

Nancy wanted to start a business that would involve her coming into people's homes to offer assessments and preventative measures. She was clearly passionate about helping people solve this problem. The issue is that most people aren't even aware of this problem. She would need to walk the Path of an Ideapreneur, meaning that she would have to first educate people about a problem and then solve it.

Working with Nancy helped me crystalize the next framework I'm about to show you, distilled from basic principles of advertising from old-time copywriting great Eugene Schwartz. It is based on the level of awareness of a prospect, from left to right:

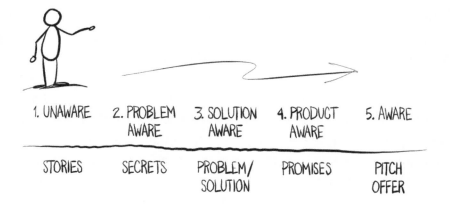

1. UNAWARE	2. PROBLEM AWARE	3. SOLUTION AWARE	4. PRODUCT AWARE	5. AWARE
STORIES	SECRETS	PROBLEM/ SOLUTION	PROMISES	PITCH OFFER

The lowest level of awareness is that a prospect is **unaware** they even have a problem. To educate the uninitiated, you must write *stories*. This is why I put such a strong emphasis on you using your Founder Story, Business Story, and Customer Story in your marketing. It ensures you have an opportunity to connect with a prospect no matter what level of awareness they are at.

When I told Nancy that I didn't really understand the problem she was trying to solve, she intuitively told me the story of how she and her family moved several times, and she discovered the problem of the RF radiation waves.

If a prospect is **problem aware**, then you should share *secrets*. For example, Nancy discovered the secret reason why she and her family were experiencing headaches. One of the lines in her pitch might be, "Do you keep getting random headaches after you've moved into a new house? Here's the real reason why!"

If a prospect is **solution aware**, they know there is a product or service out there but aren't sure who to buy from. Here, you simply re-state the problem and talk about your *solution*, which makes the prospect aware of your product.

If a prospect is **product aware**, meaning they've heard of your brand or product before, then simply make *promises* based on the dependability and reputation of your product or service.

If a prospect is **aware**, just make *direct offers*.

To summarize, when I told Nancy I didn't understand what she meant by a "healthy home," she instinctively told me the *story* of how she and her family moved several times and experienced unexplainable headaches in some of their homes. Within minutes of talking to her, I became **aware of a problem** I never heard of before, became **aware of a solution**, became **aware of her product** (her consultations), and could have been pitched an *offer* right there. This all happened in a matter of minutes.

Keep this in front of you whenever you are writing campaigns:

1. Unaware = Stories
2. Problem Aware = Secrets
3. Solution Aware = Repeat Problem / Solution
4. Product Aware = Promises
5. Aware = Pitch Your Offer

In this next section, I'm going to share a simple one-on-one script so you can head into every sales call with confidence and confidently pitch your offer. You may be wondering, "Mike, do I really need a sales call script? It feels so inauthentic. I'm much better when I improvise."

The short answer is that yes, you need a script. Years ago, the Broadway musical *Hamilton* was selling for upwards of $1,500 per ticket. If you walked a few blocks down to the improv comedy clubs, tickets were less than $30. Improvisation is cheap because you don't know what you're going to get or if the show will be any good. *Hamilton,* or any other show worth its salt, is scripted, powerful, and demands top dollar. I rest my case.

An Effective (and Ethical) Sales Call Script

I credit my friend Ray Edwards for giving me the bare bones of this approach. I've added my own spin to it and use it on nearly every single sales call. It is especially effective if I have foreknowledge of the prospect through my client intake form. Here are the bullet points, then I'll explain further.

- » "Here's what we'll cover on today's call."
- » "What caused you to reach out to me?"
- » "What do you think (or feel) is the real challenge here?"
- » "What other ways have you tried to solve this problem?"
- » "Any thoughts on why they didn't work?"
- » "Let me share how I might be able to help."
- » "Any further questions?"

Typically, I will start the call with something like, "Thanks for reaching out! Glad to chat with you today. Here's what we'll cover on the call: I'm going to ask you some questions to determine if and how I can help. Then I'll tell you what I have available. Then you can ask me any questions. When we're done, I'll ask if everything is clear. Does that sound fair?"

You must take immediate control of the call and establish the agenda. This isn't to bully anyone; it's to make the call more *effective and ethical.* The prospect will do most of the talking anyway. You are simply setting some parameters so both you and the prospect can see if taking the next steps makes sense.

I've never had anyone say no when I've started the call this way. If someone did say no, I would ask, "Is something wrong?" and if it felt like the prospect was being difficult, I would respond, "I'm sorry, I don't think we're going to be a good fit." Then I would end the call. Don't waste time.

If they agree to the parameters of the call, proceed to the next point. Depending on what they put on the client form, tie the next question to their specific situation: "What caused you to reach out to me about [your topic]?" If the prospect is a verbal processor and brain dumps on you, slow them down. Remember, keep control of the call.

Oftentimes, I will pose a clarifying question in an effort to slow them down and get the conversation back on track with the script, something like, "One moment, I just want to make sure I'm understanding what you're saying..." and then jump right in with the next question, "What do you think or feel is the real challenge here?"

Bridges Need Tension

Many sales trainers will tell you to "pour salt in the wound" of the prospect by focusing on the pain question with direct, blunt questions like, "What is your income right now?" or "How much do you need to make?"

While it's incredibly important to have your prospects focus on the pain (if there wasn't any pain, they wouldn't be talking with you in the first place), I've said time and again that marketing isn't about closing a sale, it's about opening a relationship.

And while it may feel uncomfortable to you, if the prospect is looking to deepen the relationship because they know you "get" their pain, it's your job to bridge the gap and close the sale. Yes, it can feel awkward at times, but bridges need tension!

That said, use your own discretion at how you word things. I don't like to be that blunt because it's just not my personality. If the prospect responds with a money answer, I will ask in a more thoughtful way like, "Between where you are now and where you want to be, how much money do we need to make?"

I use the word *we* because I want them to know that I'm in it with them. We're partners. We're not sitting across from each other at a negotiation table; we're sitting next to each other looking forward toward a common goal. I just want to know what that goal is.

The next two questions are subtle ways to amplify the pain: "What other ways have you tried to solve this problem?" or "Any thoughts on why they didn't work?" This will give you valuable background information so you can differentiate yourself from other solutions they have tried.

Typically, at this point the call is only at the ten- or fifteen-minute mark. Much of that will depend on how much the prospect talks and how quickly you direct the conversation. I remind you: *This is a sales call, not a therapy session or free consulting!* Allow the prospect to talk and feel understood, but don't let the call drag on. Keep it moving.

Next, share how you might be able to help them. You can talk about the solutions you offer, or better yet, talk about past clients or case studies if you have them. Oftentimes I will say, "Let me share some examples of how I might be able to help. About a year ago, I worked with someone who was also looking to start a personal brand business as a coach and speaker on the side..." If I'm permitted to share names, then I'll put a name to the case study so there is more of a connection.

You May Be the Prospect's "First"

Several times, I have come across prospects who were wanting to hire a copywriter, ghostwriter, or consultant for the very first time. In these instances, I would often ask, "What are your expectations in working with a paid copywriter?" If they responded that they didn't know what to expect, then I'd simply ask, "What do you know about the levels of copywriters?"

They would undoubtedly say they weren't familiar with the levels of copywriters out there, so I would frame my positioning by saying something like:

"A Level 10 copywriter is someone who might charge $25,000 for the initial consultation, $150,000 to write a campaign, plus a few percentage points of sales as a commission. These are guys like Dan Kennedy or Jay Abraham who write campaigns for brands like Proactiv or Icy Hot.

"A Level 1 copywriter is someone who would charge you between $1,500 to $3,000 but doesn't have any real experience. I'm a Level 7 going to a Level 8."

This would allow me to frame my fees as well as give more context to my case studies. (If you use this strategy, please tell the truth about your skill level. The last thing you want is to be completely in over your head on a project and lead the client astray.)

At this point, the prospect has done most of the talking and you will be able to tell if working with this person is a fit or not. Ask them, "Do you have any further questions right now?" If you are discussing a project, the call may essentially conclude with a Request for Proposal, or RFP. This is often the case when I take one-on-one clients because the scope of the project only becomes apparent during the call. If you are vetting someone to join a coaching group, you may tell them the fee at this point and ask them to register right there.

Your Proposal is a Marketing Tool

My policy is to have a proposal ready within three business days. The proposal is submitted with an expiration date—usually within three business days of my sending it. *Make sure you have an expiration date on your proposals.* You have better things to do than sit around and wait for someone to drag things out. This also reinforces your positioning and your brand. If it's a much bigger project that warrants a follow-up call or two, that is certainly understandable—but even my biggest projects have been very simple to set up in large part because of the way I run my sales calls.

Running a successful expertise business involves more than coaching, consulting, speaking, or freelancing. It requires clear and professional client communications and an ability to properly manage the business end of your projects. Everything is branding! The experience someone has with you on a sales call and the actual proposal document you send speaks volumes about your professionalism.

If you'd like the exact proposal templates I use to land clients, go to MikeKim.com/store. You can purchase my client intake form, official proposal template, one-page proposal (great for repeat clients), client testimonial form, and my high-ticket "pedigree" page—a hidden page (password protected) that outlines the biggest projects I've done but can't market openly. This smart little bundle is designed to help you handle every project like a pro and will save you hours of creating this stuff yourself.

Big Idea, Story, Solution: A Simple Way to Create Sticky Content

One of the most wonderful things about the different social media channels out there, and other mediums like podcasts, webinars, and YouTube videos, is that they allow us to raise the level of awareness of a prospect by telling stories and sharing our expertise.

When it comes to this kind of marketing, I try to live by a simple rule of thumb. Never tell a story without making a point, and never make a point without telling a story.

One habit I've developed is keeping a log of "big ideas"— these can be in the form of one-liners I create, maxims, or quotes from other books. I also keep a log of stories, and whenever I want to create a piece of marketing content, I use this simple sequence:

1. Big Idea
2. Story
3. Solution

The idea here is to be punchy and potent. This works really well for social media, particularly "micro-content" in the form of a video that runs under sixty seconds, or for email marketing.

One night, I was scrolling through old social media posts and noticed that several months earlier I posted, "Action cures fear." That certainly isn't a particularly unique or profound quote, but I was surprised at how many people liked the post. Since the content had been "validated" by how many people liked it, I decided to create some content around it.

At a workshop in Washington, DC, I was teaching people this simple Big Idea / Story / Solution method, so I whipped out my phone, took a selfie video, and I simply said, "Here's what we've been learning today: Action cures fear." Then I showed everyone in the background working on their first social media marketing videos and told the story of what we were doing.

You would be shocked at how many people commented on the post and sent me a private message asking me about the workshop. I was able to send them a link to the sales page for my next workshop or simply hopped on a call with them if they wanted to get more information.

Gather big ideas in an easy to access file somewhere, both your own and others' ideas. This little framework will help you keep your ideas flowing. You never know how one of them will inspire you to create content and lead to a sale.

How to Write an Irresistible Opening Line

When you write captions for social media posts, record videos for social media, or write marketing emails, it is very important to have a strong opening line.

I learned this from copywriter Ryan Schwartz (not to be confused with the late copywriter Eugene Schwartz), who I got acquainted with in the most random of ways: Ryan's life partner, Sue, was my assistant for the early part of my business. Little did I know her boyfriend was a top copywriter in the internet marketing space! The marketing gods must have ordained our acquaintance on my behalf because he taught me this method:

1. Write the phrase, "I never thought it was possible, but..."
2. Complete the thought.
3. Delete the "I never thought it was possible, but..."

The first phrase keeps you from overthinking and gets your mind in a creative space to think of surprising or even shocking things. Here's a real-world application from one of my own marketing emails:

> STEP 1: "I never thought it was possible, but most email marketing is weak." (I tried to think of a metaphor for something weak.)
>
> STEP 2: "I never thought it was possible, but most email marketing is weaker than Shaquille O'Neal's free throw game." (Shaquille O'Neal, simply known as Shaq, is a Hall of Fame basketball player who was notorious for his terrible free throw shooting.)
>
> STEP 3: "~~I never thought it was possible, but~~ most email marketing is weaker than Shaquille O'Neal's free throw game."
>
> RESULT: "Most email marketing is weaker than Shaquille O'Neal's free throw game."

The response to that email was off the charts. Many readers personally responded saying how funny it was and how it caused them to read the rest of the email. This is a good thing! You want people to feel something in your marketing collateral, whether it's humor, joy, inspiration, outrage, or any range of emotions. When your marketing becomes predictable, that's when it becomes boring—and eventually ignored.

The Five Levels of Awareness in an Actual Campaign

I would be remiss if I didn't provide an example of how I weave in the five levels of awareness into an actual campaign.

These are the subject lines of an email campaign I wrote. The "Bootcamp" refers to a free three-video training I promoted on social media. To register for the training, a prospect had to submit their email address, adding them to my list. Once on my list, I was able to send more content directly and pitch the program.

You will find the corresponding "level of awareness" content in parentheses next to the subject line. Email #1 was simply the confirmation email for the three-video course, so the campaign really starts with email #2.

1. Welcome to the Brand You Bootcamp!
2. Bootcamp Session 1 + The Three Yous (*secrets*)
3. Bootcamp Session 2: The Two Types of Entrepreneurs (*secrets*)
4. How Much Money Do You Need for a Career Pivot? (*story, secrets*)
5. Bootcamp Session 3: How To (Properly) Identify Your Ideal Client (*story, secrets*)
6. A 36-hour "Flash Open" (*problem / solution*)
7. Registration is now live! (*direct offer*)
8. Pivot from day job to dream job in the same industry (*story, secrets, direct offer*)
9. Fired from day job, start a coaching business (*story, secrets, direct offer*)
10. Success is more certain when... (*direct offer*)

You can see that the direct offers start at email #7 because by that point the prospect has seen a lot of content from the campaign. The key to this campaign was the combination of *story*, *secrets*, and *direct offer* as seen in Email #8 and Email #9.

This process reduced the fatigue of getting pounded with offers and allowed prospects to re-enter a narrative and connect with stories. I took the time to tell some transformation stories from past clients, distill them into snackable tips, and make the pitch—all in one email. Here is the first of those emails, Email #8:

One of the biggest questions I get about [Program Name] is:

"Is it *really* possible to pivot into my own full-time business?"

Here's a story that illustrates exactly what is possible...

Joseph B. used to work at a lawyer marketing company doing website development, online marketing, and print advertising.

He always dreamed of running his own business from home... but with a wife and two young children, making that kind of transition had a lot of ramifications:

1.   Income uncertainty
2.   The transition of working at an office to working at home
3.   Where to find consistent clients
4.   How to create multiple revenue streams (not just client work)
5.   How to bring up the topic of quitting your job with your spouse!

Joseph enrolled in [Program Name] and applied a key takeaway from one of the strategies inside the program:

Make your employer your first client.

Because Joseph wanted to stay in the same industry (marketing), he was able to leverage his position with his employer and transition into a part-time or contractor role.

Then he used the strategies in [Program Name] to set up a minimum viable platform and put himself out to the market *doing the same kind of work* he did for his employer.

Imagine getting paid multiple times for the same kind of work, over and over again. That's what Joseph did, and he has now been full-time in his own business for the past *four* years:

[client headshot with picture and quote]

Joseph repeatedly told me that this was "the best course I've ever taken" and texted me:

"It's not only that it was the best course, you taught complete and complex ideas in an extremely easy way. I got real results from the course. It is gold."

Life has come full circle for us—last year, when I was hired by [Client] on a marketing project, I hired Joseph to run their online ads.

He is still working with them even though my contract has expired—and it's a testament to the power of what happens when you have clarity on your brand and relationships in your network.

If you apply yourself, then [Program Name] can give you the plan to move forward.

The "flash open" for [Program Name] is now available at this link:

Click here to register now »

(There's also a payment plan.)

The offer is only available for 24 more hours…

Click here to register now »

I received numerous responses from buyers that this email was the reason they purchased the program. Is that true? Of course not. The reason they purchased is because they were nurtured through a thoughtful campaign, but this email helped close the sale.

Big Rocks vs. Small Pebbles: How to Create Annual Marketing Campaigns

I want to close this chapter by sharing a way you can get above the day-to-day scramble and get a 30,000-foot view of your pitches through the course of a year.

I firmly believe you need to have some sort of a big push at least two to three times a year, preferably three. That way, the interim periods of time can be used to create content and nurture prospects into whatever you are promoting.

One thing every business owner must understand is the importance of throwing big rocks into the pond to make waves. The phrase "publicity stunt" has come to receive a bad rap, but it's a vital part of marketing.

A weekly blog post or podcast is great, but those won't really make waves unless a particular content piece goes viral. Daily posts on social media are great, but they're more like pebbles you throw into a pond. It makes for a cool sound, but it doesn't make waves—at least when it comes to sales.

At some point, you need to pick up a big rock, throw that sucker into the water, and make a big splash! When I started out, the big rocks were my first webinars, my first virtual summit, and my first product launch. Webinars, summits, and product launches create waves. Even if no one buys—they are, in and of themselves, publicity stunts. People take notice because you're doing a big promotion—and the perception is that you are doing something much bigger than what your own numbers may say.

If you run a more traditional business such as a brick-and-mortar or professional services business (law, hair salon, restaurant, etc.), then creating waves takes on a different bent.

When I worked my day job as CMO of the educational company, we often did "blitzes." These were a series of live events stacked throughout a given month (usually March) to generate an influx of customers for the summer. These open houses and workshops created buzz because we were promoting something that had scarcity and urgency. We plastered the advertising everywhere, and the community was "blitzed" with these promotions.

I've met many people who hide behind content and never dare to do their first webinar or launch. You have to take risks and throw some big rocks into the water in addition to the small pebbles. Here's a sample marketing strategy using my business as an example. The small pebbles:

1. Weekly podcast episodes
2. Weekly YouTube videos
3. Monthly blog posts on marketing and branding
4. Emails to my list twice a week
5. Social media posts across all platforms 2x per week

Who knows, maybe one of the pieces of content goes viral—but you can't build a marketing strategy around hope alone. Please don't misunderstand; pebbles are important. You can't build a foundation on just big rocks because they're too jagged. You need pebbles to fill in the gaps, but neither can you build an entire foundation of just pebbles.

As for big rocks, I do these only a few times a year. I divide the year into thirds, not quarters. I plan for three four-month blocks: January–April, May–August, and September–December. An example:

1. **January–April:** Launch a free online coaching group to generate buzz and grow my email list, then sell a charter ninety-day private coaching group to registrants.

2. **May–August:** Host a small workshop. Offer the workshop ticket at a lower rate to my coaching group students and fill the rest of the seats with an offer to the open market at the regular registration fee. Collect video testimonials, post pictures of the workshop on social media (thereby creating buzz), and record the teaching sessions. At the event, promote another private coaching group to attendees.

3. **September–December:** Launch an online course made up of the video recordings from the workshop. Take the best coaching calls from the charter coaching group and rerecord that content into videos to complete the course. Take video clips from the workshop and create micro-content for social media.

One thing simply feeds the next. Each big rock generates revenue, creates buzz, gives me content for the next rock, and builds deeper relationships with my clients. Just imagine undergirding all these big rocks with the small pebbles I mentioned earlier. Now that's a strong foundation!

You may wonder why I don't do a "big rock" campaign four times a year (and use ninety-day quarters). It's because ninety days is much too short a time window for my kind of business to put the kind of marketing muscle behind a promotion that a big rock deserves. Not only will you wear out, your market will often feel like you're scattered. One day you're promoting a course, and the next day you turn around and you're hawking a book, and then a mastermind group, and so forth. I've found a big rock every four months works well.

As your business grows, your big rocks will change over time. When I first started, my big rocks included pitching my copywriting services (I was nervous!), hosting my first webinar, or launching my podcast. Now those things are a given because my business has grown and the rocks have become bigger.

Pitch or Perish!

Regardless of what constitutes big rocks or small pebbles right now, you must consistently do things that will keep you top of mind with your market. In order to attract bigger clients, bigger stages, and more opportunities, you must build your body of work. You can't build a reputation on what you're going to do.

I'll never forget one of the early webinars I hosted. This took place back in 2015, when I was doing my first-ever product launch for a course I was promoting.

I decided to host webinars to promote the course and wanted to test different times. I tried one at 8 p.m. ET, 2 p.m. ET, and (gulp!) 11 a.m. ET. The first two time slots were really well attended, and I made a good number of sales. The 11 a.m. ET time slot, much to my chagrin, only resulted in two people showing up!

I had to make a decision then and there. Was I hosting this webinar simply to sell a course, or was I doing it to truly add value to whoever attended? I decided I would bring the same energy to these two people as I did to the two hundred people who attended the previous night at 8 p.m. What happened? One out of the two people purchased the course, a 50% conversion rate!

I share this story with you because it's easy to think that I'm some "expert" who is spouting off a bunch of advice to you. No, friend. I've walked the Path you're walking. I've had my fair share of quirky (and sometimes discouraging) moments in business—like this webinar story.

Regardless of what happens, we have to keep going. We have to keep pitching. We have to keep throwing big rocks into the pond. Next time you get a bit anxious about putting yourself out there and pitching an offer, just remember—even two people attending a webinar isn't a failure. I still get butterflies when making offers, but I continually remind myself that I have a duty to help people and a duty to my business to keep it afloat.

Whenever I get squeamish about pitching offers, I remind myself that I've been generous in giving so much of my expertise away for free, have poured untold hours into honing my skills and building relationships, and I've been *truthful* in my marketing. Pitch or perish!

CHAPTER TEN

Partners:
Relationships
Are Rocket Ships

When I was in my early twenties, I was asked by my church to host a guest speaker coming into town. This gentleman had been a regular guest for the past year, and I got to know him during his visits. My job was to pick him up from the airport, drive him to the hotel, and get anything he needed to make his stay more comfortable. I was tasked to do this for nearly the entire time he was in town.

This man was one of the most unique people I had ever met. He had a powerful presence about him, and no wonder—he carried the title of "King" of one of the tribes in eastern Ghana.

The conversations I had with him in the car, in the hallways, and during meals were priceless—they were just as impactful, if not more, than what he shared from behind a pulpit. While driving him around, he would sometimes take important phone calls with world leaders, and I was able to hear how he spoke to these people. One day, after finishing a call with someone at the United Nations, he said something to me that I still remember to this day: "Son, you are talented, but you must understand—life is 10% *what* you know, and 90% *who* you know."

Honestly, I didn't believe him at the time. I was young, had my entire future ahead of me, and truly believed that talent was enough. As the years passed, I slowly started to realize he was right.

This is one of the reasons I've been such a strong advocate of building relationships as a part of building your brand. We've spent the majority of our time talking about how to use marketing to open relationships with prospects. Now let's turn our attention toward building relationships with partners and friends because lone rangers don't last long in this business. Relationships are rocket ships. One of the people who has exemplified that the most is my friend Paul Martinelli.

"Partner Up, Collaborate Across, Mentor Around"

Paul Martinelli has helped build some of the biggest names in the personal development space, having worked directly with people such as John Maxwell, Bob Procter, and Dr. Daniel Amen, and he was directly responsible for tens of millions of dollars in sales of their intellectual property.

One of the reasons he has been so successful is because, rather than just a singular strategy, Paul advocates for a three-pronged approach to building relationships: "Partner up, collaborate across, and mentor around." When Paul told me this, I had a lightbulb moment because he gave me language around what I was doing in an "unconsciously competent" manner!

But I sort of did it in reverse.

When I started my blog in 2013, I didn't know a single person in the online marketing space. As I started to walk the Path I shared with you in chapter two, I stumbled upon a few things that accelerated my progress, grew my brand, and eventually attracted partners and collaborators.

Looking back, I can see how these things all fit together, but it's important I share my initial baby steps with you first. Then I'll close this chapter with how I leveraged my small but growing brand to partner up, collaborate across, and mentor around—to attract exponentially greater opportunities very quickly.

That said, I cannot emphasize this enough: All of this is contingent on you building your brand as someone people want to be associated with. When you become self-important, you will be tolerated rather than celebrated. Now, let's start with the first strategy I employed when starting out: becoming someone else's best case study.

Strategy #1: Become Someone Else's Best Case Study

Keep in mind that every big-name expert out there was once a beginner. Every leader started out as a follower. Every guru was once a student. No matter how "big" someone may seem, he or she is still a *person* and their core desires remain the same. So, what do these big names really want? It's simple. They want publicity or profits.

The downside is that when you are first starting out, you may not have a large enough following to garner them extra publicity or profits. That means we have to think of different ways to give them what they want and contribute to them beyond what everyone else is doing. One of the easiest ways to do this is by becoming someone else's best case study.

I mentioned earlier that one of my early online mentors was leadership author Michael Hyatt. When I started my blog in 2013, I wanted to learn how to do it more effectively and simply googled something like "how to blog." Michael was teaching a lot of blogging techniques at the time, so he came up in the search results and I started reading his content. It turned out he had a podcast, so I listened to it religiously while commuting to my day job.

Eventually, I joined one of Michael's courses, a monthly membership site that cost about $30 a month. That was all I could justify at the time because I wanted to prove to myself I could stick to blogging before spending more money. I got to work and did pretty much everything he said. I was active in the members community, shared his content on social media, and showed up to nearly every monthly Q&A call for a year.

Michael had hundreds of thousands of followers on social media, a top-ranked business podcast, and hundreds of thousands of people on his email list. But as a member of his program, I became just one of several thousand. By showing up on his coaching calls, I became just one of a few hundred. By taking action on what he taught, I became one of just a few.

You must understand that these creators are looking much more closely at their students and customers than they are at the general public. Over several months, he took notice of me and started to share my blog posts on his own social media channels. Michael's followers started to take notice of me. They wanted to know, "Who is this Mike Kim guy that keeps getting his blog posts shared by Michael Hyatt?"

Eventually, I was asked to share my story on a promotional webinar Michael was hosting for his program. It was an opportunity to be a part of bringing him publicity for his program, but another thing happened as well: By simple association with someone of Michael's caliber, other influencers started to take notice of me.

Strategy #2: Invest in More Exclusive Opportunities

When connecting with influencers, it's important to do this with someone who still maintains a more personal touch with their audience. A global figure in your industry who has amassed a huge following probably isn't looking at their customers and clients in the same way as someone on an upward ascent. If they are, those opportunities will often require a bigger investment of money.

I shared the story about Michael Hyatt, but his program was just about a year old at that time. In the years since, he has written numerous books, shifted into doing leadership development and productivity instead of teaching blogging, and his audience has grown tremendously. The same strategy wouldn't work for where he is in his business and level of influence now.

The big question to ask yourself at this point is, "What is more important, time or money?"

For me, it was time. I didn't want to toil for two, three, or four years just doing my thing and trying to make progress on my own. I needed to invest in more than just my personal or professional development; I needed to invest in my professional *network*. That's when I started to look for opportunities that would help me hit all three of those things: personal development, professional development, and professional network.

One of the best ways to do this is investing in more exclusive opportunities, like coaching groups, mastermind groups, and smaller in-person events.

While taking Michael's program, I stumbled upon a video teaching from inside the group by a guy named Ray Edwards. Ray was a copywriting and marketing consultant, and I immediately felt connected to him. Today, Ray is a dear friend, but back then, he didn't know me at all. I looked for ways to "connect with connectors," and as fate would have it, sometime later Ray offered an exclusive high-ticket mastermind group. I met incredible people there, some of whom have become dear friends and partners in various business endeavors.

As my network has grown over the years, I've realized this simple principle: The good people know good people who know more good people.

Be the Jelly to Someone Else's Peanut Butter

About a year later, Ray created a marketing program and was looking for affiliate partners. Publicity and profit were important to him. By that time, my brand was slowly growing between my blog and podcast, and I agreed to co-promote his program and made it my mission to be one of the top five promoters among his joint venture partners. Long story short, I finished first. That granted me even more exposure, not just to his followers but to the other affiliate partners. They wanted to know who I was, and that resulted in even more connections. This high-level validation brought me a tremendous amount of confidence.

Coming in first place was unexpected for me because my list size compared to the other participants was paltry. The results came down to the wire, with me beating out one of the legends in the internet marketing space. That certainly put me on that guy's radar too.

So, how did I do it? The key to enticing people to purchase a product through your link is to offer bonuses *unique to you*. Earn the right to make a recommendation. Making a good product is the job of the promoter. Creating an irresistible package is the job of the affiliate. Were I to distill affiliate internet marketing promotions into one simple principle, it would be this: Make your offer the jelly to someone else's peanut butter.

The product I was promoting was for copywriting. While I am a copywriter, it wouldn't make much sense to offer copywriting bonuses in addition to the main product. That's just heaping more peanut butter onto the bread. Instead, I tried to think of what the jelly would be, and I chose personal branding.

Many people buy Ray's program to hone their copywriting skills, but many of them also want to become full-time freelance copywriters. This was the gap I could fill. Offering them branding help on how to market themselves, how to market their skills, and how to make industry connections turned out to be the perfect complement.

All this to say, please be selective about who you partner with and promote. Your name and reputation will ultimately be on the line, so it's important to think through who you choose to align yourself with. I only promote people and products I genuinely find valuable, and I work extremely hard to earn the right to make recommendations to my followers. With earning their trust comes the responsibility to keep it.

Many of These Folks Just Went to School Together

I meet many people who complain that successful people are only interested in other successful people. They don't like this supposed "elitism."

But have you ever caught up with an old friend you grew up with in school, sports, or church? There's a special rapport between people who "went to school together." Now imagine coming up through the ranks of entrepreneurship together and ending up in a place of freedom and success.

Many of the experts you may want to partner with actually got their start around the same time. They're not being elitist. They're just "school friends." They are, as Paul Martinelli says, collaborating *across*. They have years of trust and rapport with one another that you could never replicate with them. Of course, once in a while, you can partner with them. But it's very hard to break in unless you do something very noticeable.

That's why it's even more important to grow your own network of people you are coming up with. You need others you can create your own camaraderie with and continue to do things that your peers take notice of. You've got to consistently up your game with each other because remember, as the influence of another person grows, so do their standards.

One of the guys I "went to school with" in entrepreneurship was Jared Easley. We first met at a conference, and I started listening to his podcast, *Starve the Doubts*. I decided to write a blog post about why I liked his show, and to my surprise, he took notice and we just started chatting.

Little did I know that behind the scenes, Jared was starting a conference for podcasters. He was just Jared to me at the time, but his conference, Podcast Movement, went on to become one of the largest podcasting events in the United States. He invited me to speak at the inaugural conference, and that was actually my first-ever business speaking event.

While we knew each other from our days starting out, he has grown his business and influence. He is still very down to earth, but there are other things he needs to take into consideration now that his event has grown. It would be tough to get a speaking engagement there if you've never spoken anywhere before—his conference is now a staple in the industry and has been running for years. Jared has business partners who make decisions collectively with him—he can't just say, "Hey guys, I want to help my friend Mike by giving him a speaking slot. He's never spoken at a business event before, but I'm sure he'll be great." I can continue being friends with him, but if I want to continue collaborating with him on a professional level, I've got to meet higher standards.

That's why I'm still investing in myself (you might be shocked at how much money I spend on coaching), and I'm committed to always upping my game. And that's why I'm willing to "pay it forward" for others who are growing in how they work, learn, and serve.

Strategy #3: Contribute Your Skills to Cultivate Partnerships

I'm often asked how I've built so many connections with influential people in my industry. When I look back at my career, the most significant connections I made came through me lending my skills to other businesses and building relationships with them through our work together.

Back in chapter seven, we talked about the five plays of the personal brand: speaking, coaching, consulting, writing, and productizing. The key for me was to approach relationships with the appropriate skill to help them build *their* business.

In 2018, I worked with one of leadership expert John Maxwell's companies as a marketing strategist and copywriter. If I approached them as a coach or speaker and wanted to directly partner with them outright, I would have been a competitor because John is also a coach and speaker—and a much bigger name than me. I would have been perceived as someone trying to leech off of his influence.

But because I had a noncompeting skill that could *contribute* to their business, I ended up spending a considerable amount of time with John and his team. Moreover, my personal brand positioned me as more than simply a contractor for hire. Rather, I was seen as a collaborator and partner because not only did I level up their marketing campaigns, I had a thriving podcast and a strong network of influencers that I could bring to the table. While I felt as if working with The John Maxwell Team was certainly a "partner up" for me, they saw little old me as a "partner up" because of my skills, influence, and network.

Before long, they had me onstage at their events, teaching their audience online. They even promoted several of my courses, which resulted in sales that were five times the amount they paid me for my contract! But could you imagine if I came into that relationship with no personal brand? With no connections, platform, or products to speak of? What a squandered opportunity that would have been! Yet I see so many contractors do this, all because they didn't take the time to build a personal brand, grow their network, and earn influence. I am not exaggerating when I say *this breaks my heart*.

Strategy #4: The Epic Breakfast

One of the best ways to build rapport with others and grow your network is to host a meetup. Several times early in my career, I hosted small, intimate events, and it has helped me build great relationships, which my friends and I have dubbed "The Epic Breakfast."

This is an invite-only small gathering that I usually host at breakfast during conferences I attend or am speaking at. Breakfast works because, first, it's outside the scheduled parameters of a conference or meeting. You don't want to host your own event when an actual conference is happening—that is not a good way to make friends.

Second, scheduling breakfast ensures there is an end time to your meetup. I've turned down many dinner networking events simply because I didn't want to get dragged into a potentially painful and endless night of networking. Breakfast ensures we are in and out on a time clock.

Oftentimes, I will enlist the help of one or two other colleagues who have their own connections at the event and ask them to personally invite a few people to the breakfast. Once someone hears that another person of some influence will attend, they almost always want to come. Some folks have asked me directly, "Who is going to be there? If such-and-such comes, I will definitely come." Even though this sounds like I'm herding people for a high school party, I don't mind. It's just how people think. They want to know it's going to be worth their time.

Normally, I cap the meetup at fifteen people because of the way I arrange the meal. Having more people than this can make the day go long, so it's important you maintain control of who is invited and gets a seat. By the way, I always pay for the breakfast. Don't invite people out and then make them pay.

At the meal, we follow the "one conversation" rule, and I facilitate the meeting. The "only one conversation at the table" rule gives everyone a chance to speak and prevents the chatterboxes from monopolizing the conversation. I'm actually more of an introvert, so if I'm in a room full of chatty people, I usually shut down. This little rule empowers the introverts at the table, and I assure you they will appreciate the gesture.

I usually open with a short welcome, housekeeping details (like where the restrooms are), I share the "one conversation" rule, and I let people know we will end on time.

We usually start with a short self-introduction (name, where you're from, what you do) and an icebreaker question. At one meetup I co-hosted in Nashville, our icebreaker question was to share the title of the last book we read with the tag at the end "with a chainsaw." People had a good laugh. It was funny to hear, "I'm Mike Kim, a marketing strategist from New Jersey, and the last book I read was *How to Win Friends and Influence People... With a Chainsaw.*" If you consider that there are fifteen people at the table and each one takes a turn, you've probably already spent fifteen to twenty minutes together.

Once everyone introduces themselves, I start by posing one question for the group, answer the question myself, and then call on someone else to answer the question. Once that person answers, she calls on another person, and this goes on until everyone has answered. This format keeps everyone on their toes and allows their names to be heard an additional time.

For example, it might be my turn to call on someone and I'll be able to say, "I call on—sorry, what was your name again?" all without being awkward. If you facilitate this properly, it is actually a very powerful experience because you let people know it's okay not to know each other's names right away.

Once a person shares their answer to the question, that gives the others at the table even more context as to who they are and what they do. Oftentimes, people stick around and continue talking at the conclusion of the breakfast, and they often talk about what they shared during the breakfast. If you do just one question and give each person a minute or two to share, another half hour has passed. I have never gotten past three total questions at the breakfast, including the introduction. This can run a total of an hour to an hour and a half, and everyone can leave and make it in time for the opening session of the conference or meeting.

When you plan your questions, it is important to know your audience. You should have an idea about who is going to be there since it's an invite-only gathering. It may be a crowd who can get very open and vulnerable, or it may be a crowd of folks who are rather closed off. These questions have been very good for the groups I've hosted; you may well have your own.

1.   What is giving you the most energy right now in your business or personal life?

2.   What are you working on that really excites you?

3.   What is one habit or practice that has improved your quality of life?

4.   What is something you learned in the last three months that you wish you knew three years ago?

These questions are intentionally open-ended. They give room for people to discuss things from a professional standpoint, like a new project, client, or opportunity. Or they may talk about something personal, like a new exercise routine, family update, or their perspective on work-life balance. It's completely left to their discretion. The important thing is that these questions focus the conversation on something positive and life-giving, which is what most successful entrepreneurs or business leaders focus on anyway.

After the breakfast is done, see if you can snap a group photo with everyone there. Some of them may share the photo on social media, and because you were the one who made it happen, the photo will elevate your brand across your network.

The Strategic Selfie

Speaking of snapping photos, this is a new frontier for many people, and there are great ways to help you build connections that are new and creative. (I operate in a much more social media-driven industry, so use this method with your own discretion.)

Let's take a quick look at a few things that may help you build relationships and partnerships with the people you meet.

I talked about the Sadistic Selfie, which were photos I took of myself looking miserable so I could remind myself there was more to life than what I was doing at the time. Well, this is the opposite: the Strategic Selfie. Instead of carrying business cards, I simply do the following to make an impression and then follow up.

1.   Take a selfie with the person I want to connect with.

2.   Email the photo to them directly because it's much easier to recognize each other via photo than a business card. I get their email address, and I include my phone number in the email.

3. Post the selfie on social media, tag their accounts, and tag the event.

4. Follow up in the same email thread I sent with our initial photo after the event.

I've done this with a number of people I've met to great effect. I understand that in some industries, business cards are still the norm, so I leave this to your discretion, and by all means please do not be creepy when asking to take the photo with someone! But don't miss the point: Having your picture taken with someone is usually taken as a compliment. And posting that you've met someone is a great way to connect with them and interact.

But this isn't about having your picture taken with a "celebrity." This is about "opening a relationship" with someone you would like to get to know. People don't want to feel used... but they do want to connect.

Strategy #5: Make the People You Serve Significant

It's easy to think that you need to have a big following or considerable influence before you pull the trigger and start doing "big" things, but I've found the opposite is true.

In late 2017, I hosted my first business event called *Influence & Impact*. This was a small (forty people), invitation-only event that I hosted just minutes from where I was living at the time in northern New Jersey. I've said several times that business is nothing more than solving a problem for a profit, and whenever I launch any new initiative, I ask myself, "What is the big problem I want to solve?"

When marketing *Influence & Impact*, I called or emailed these folks and said, "Here's the big problem I want to solve: I have some high-caliber friends from different circles of life who need to meet one another. I'm going to do something about it. There are two or three people at an event I'm hosting that you need to meet. Will you come?" My pitch was that simple.

During my opening remarks at the event, I said that the reason we were all gathering together was because there were people in my life who I knew needed to meet one another. The problem is that the only way they would ever all be in the same room was at my funeral, and that I would prefer to be alive! After a few nervous chuckles (everyone was familiar with my dry sense of humor), I told my friends that I wanted them to leave the event with three things:

1. Belief
2. Clarity
3. Connections

I said those things repeatedly during our two days together, and it's no surprise that people said those three things were exactly what they received by the end of the event. That's intentional branding. It's important to equip people with the language you want them to use to describe your work.

It may seem as if I'm giving you a blueprint to host your own event, but more than that, I'm trying to help you understand that you don't need to be "big" to do this. My email list was very small at the time I hosted this event. My podcast was just a few years old. I didn't have big-name clients or big-time coaching programs, and I certainly didn't have the budget to pay industry-leading speakers to grace my stage. Every speaker at that event was a friend, colleague, or someone I was personally coaching in one of my mastermind groups. This was the first-ever public speaking engagement for many of these folks. I personally coached many of them through their presentation and was able to give them a professional video recording of their speech that they could use in their marketing.

This was the gift I wanted to give to those particular people. I wanted to make them significant. I wanted my guests to be significant. I wanted the event to elevate others, not me. And yet in doing so, my brand—and yes, my influence and impact—grew exponentially. The ripple effects from that event, and so many of the other things I've done in the years since, have been incredible. Many of these folks have partnered in business together, and some have become the best of friends.

Here's my challenge to you: Don't look for a significant place to serve; make where you serve significant. A candle loses nothing by lighting another candle. Don't look at who isn't at your party; be present with the ones who are there with you. Don't just look to gain more influence; make a positive impact on those who you carry influence with. If you look just a bit deeper, you will find that you have more resources, assets, and value than you think.

Friend, there is no excuse. You can do every single thing I've outlined in this chapter, and if I can be a bit more personal for a moment, I hosted *Influence & Impact* on the heels of a painful marital separation. I was able to power through simply because I truly wanted to help my friends. If you truly believe in solving a problem for people and apply just a bit of branding "elbow grease," incredible things can happen.

Become Someone People Want to Partner With

We started this chapter talking about how to partner with influential people, but here's the cool thing—when you build your brand according to the *Brand You Blueprint,* you become the person other people want to partner with. You have a point of view. You have authentic and powerful personal stories. Your positioning is clear, your platforms are growing, and you have products that solve real-world problems.

People may not be able to articulate exactly what draws them to partner with you, but you know the answer. It's because you are the brand. You've done the hard work. You've paid the price. You've walked the Path. Now you're ready to step into and leverage partnerships that will skyrocket your influence, impact, and income.

Closing

As we close, I want to remind you of what I hoped you would feel while reading this book: *"Finally! This is what I've been looking for. I can do this."*

As you've heard me say multiple times now, marketing isn't about closing a sale; it's about opening a relationship. I hope I've exemplified this by sharing ideas, stories, and examples with you in an authentic way. I hope I've communicated warmth and hope. I hope you can see that you don't need to rely on image, flamboyance, and pizzazz to make an impact. I hope, if I ever host a literal campfire, you'll want to come!

Most of all, I hope I've helped you dig deep and realize that *you are the brand.*

I'm repeating myself here, but it bears repeating: It's going to take work (and a bit of vulnerability) on your part. It's easy to think, "Great! Once I have this all figured out, I'll start." Nope. I'm going to ask you to start and figure it out as you go. The more you put yourself out there, the more you will start to discover yourself.

I also mentioned that this book is meant to serve as a blueprint. You've learned some new things, but my hope is that you will come back to this book over and over again as a guide to keep you on track.

A Word about Rejection

It pains me to say this, but I can't let you go without mentioning the issue of rejection.

The journey to building a personal brand business is like any other business: There are ups and downs, good days and bad. You have to fight through the hard days in order to earn the best days.

We often take any kind of rejection as a *personal* rejection. It's not. Believe me, I've spent my fair share of time getting hung up about what someone says of me online, unsubscribing from my email list, or unfollowing me on social media. Whenever you are in someone else's head, no one else is taking care of yours. Focus on what matters.

I don't take that stuff personally anymore because while I strive to be authentic and real, those people don't know me personally. To most people in this world, I'm just another "character" on the internet. When someone says no to me, they're not rejecting Mike Kim the person. They're saying, "Mike Kim the Personal Branding Guy isn't what I need or want right now."

Outside of my family and friends, humanity at large doesn't know me in a way that should ever make me feel *personally* rejected. That privilege is reserved for very few people in my life, and I hope you will feel the same way about yourself as well.

The bottom line: You can't always control what happens *to* you, but you can control what happens *in* you. So, play all out. Leave it all on the field. Push your limits to see what you're made of. Don't hold back. Don't let others take away your peace.

Open Doors for Others

I want to encourage you in one final way. Open doors for people. Give people chances they'd otherwise never get. Leverage your influence to launch others into their calling. Write recommendations that give people what they could never get on their own. Refer. Brag. Name drop others on their behalf. You don't have to wait until you're famous, wealthy, or a household name to do this. You can do it now.

Influence is currency. It's meant to flow. The more you use it for others, the more you get. The stingiest, most small-minded people I've met aren't just cheap with money—they are cheap in spirit. An abundance of money will not fix a poverty of spirit.

Just imagine what the world would be like if no one cared about getting the credit. Sure, some of the people you open doors for will throw you under the bus or forget you. Keep doing it anyway. When you open doors for others, more doors open for you. You become a connector. Your business becomes something people can build a campfire around.

Yet opening doors will also keep you humble.

I have spent a lot of time in New York City. Many buildings still have a doorman standing there patiently day after day. They are there solely to help you and make your life easier as you go into the building.

The sheer concept of an arrogant doorman is foolish. That's why opening doors for others works. Even if a doorman feels passed over, he sees everything. He knows everyone. He is observant, patient, well-mannered, and knows more than people think he does.

If you don't mind seeing others succeed and do better than you, nothing can stop you. You'll grow your network the real way. You'll become a connector the real way. You'll prosper the real way. You'll be unstoppable, unforgettable, and influential because no one can lord over the one who is generous.

Stay on the Path

Friend, it's been a real honor to be a small part of your journey. There are days (sometimes seasons) where fighting for clarity can feel as if you're grasping the wind or squeezing water: The more you try, the more it seems to elude you. Other days, it can feel like you're walking through a heavy fog trying to grab a twig, branch, or just anything to hold on to. It can be frustrating, but you'll never find your way out of the fog by just sitting where you are and waiting for the weather to clear up.

Remember the Path I showed you back in the beginning? Stay the course and keep doing the work. Get the reps in. Find every opportunity to hone the five plays of speaking, writing, consulting, coaching, and productizing. As you walk the Path, you'll sharpen your abilities and attract new opportunities, partners, and friends.

My hope is that what I've shared in this book has filled you with inspiration, motivated you to take action, and equipped you with new knowledge and skills. Most importantly, my hope is that this book has helped you see yourself in a new light.

It might be hard to see yourself in a different light right now, but believe me, there's something special happening. Keep walking the Path.

My final charge to you: Live your message, love your work, leave your mark on the world. Remember, you are the brand.

To your success,
Mike Kim

P. S. In the next section, I've recapped the questions I've posed in each of the chapters to help you move forward. I've also included my own "Press Kit," which incorporates various elements of the marketing collateral I've shared with you throughout the book. The press kit has been invaluable in saving me time and helping me pitch myself to get new publicity, such as podcast interviews and speaking engagements. Take and tweak for your own use.

P. P. S. Remember I told you I hated it when other books said, "Decide what problem you want to solve and go find clients" without giving any concrete examples or scripts?

If you go to YouAreTheBrandBook.com, you can get editable versions of the templates and swipe files in this book, along with exercises to turn your "ideas into actions." I've laid it all out for you step by step.

As the great Yoda said, "Do. Or do not. There is no try."

Questions

Chapter 1: Who Do You Have to Become?

1. Which general market you are in: health, wealth, or relationships?

Chapter 2: Which One Are You?

1. Are you more of a How-To-Preneur or an Ideapreneur?
2. Do you prefer a horizontal focus, a vertical focus, or a blend of both?
3. Does differentiating between demographics and psychographics provide more clarity for you?

Chapter 3: Point of View

1. What pisses you off?
2. What breaks your heart?
3. What's the big problem you're trying to solve?

Chapter 4: Personal Stories

1. What is your Founder Story?
2. What is your Business Story?
3. What is your Customer Story?

Make sure to use the Introduction, Inciting Incident, Resolution approach to writing all three.

Chapter 5: Platform

I mentioned that my year-by-year focus looked something like this:

2013—The Year of the Blog
2014—The Year of the Podcast
2015—The Year of Group Coaching
2016—The Year of the Product Launch
2017—The Year of the Live Event
2018—The Year of Speaking
2019—The Year of Video
2020—The Year of Book Writing
2021—The Year of Book Launching

What aspect of your platform are you focusing on building this year?

Chapter 6: Positioning

I mentioned that I teach strategy to non-marketers, which helped me draw a distinction between other brands out there. Who are your closest competitors?

Chapter 7: Products

1. What do you want me to pay you for?
2. Which one of my friends would you like to talk to?

Chapter 8: Pricing

1. What is your "Traffic from Hell" hourly rate?

Chapter 9: Pitch

1. What are the three "big rocks" in your annual marketing campaign this year?

Chapter 10: Partners

1. I outlined five strategies you can use to attract partners: Which of these do you plan to employ in the next 90 days?

-   Strategy #1: Become someone else's best case study.
-   Strategy #2: Invest in more exclusive opportunities.
-   Strategy #3: Contribute your skills to cultivate partnerships.
-   Strategy #4: Host your own Epic Breakfast at conferences and other events.
-   Strategy #5: Make the people you serve significant.

Press Kit Template

As more opportunities started to present themselves, I found myself spending an inordinate amount of time sending the same information to podcasters, event coordinators, and virtual summit hosts. I finally wised up and put one of my professional bios and some suggested interview questions onto a page on my site, along with my headshot, logo, and current social media handles. I've probably saved hours per month since creating this press kit template.

Chances are the content of my press kit will change, but I've put the most recent one here for you to take and tweak. You can find the live page at MikeKim.com/presskit.

* * *

Mike Kim is a marketing strategist, direct-response copywriter, and author of *You Are the Brand: The 8-Step Blueprint to Showcase Your Unique Expertise and Build a Highly Profitable, Personally Fulfilling Business*. He has been hired by some of today's most influential thought leader brands and spoken at industry-leading events including Social Media Marketing World, Podcast Movement, and Tribe Conference.

For years he was the Chief Marketing Officer of a successful multi-million-dollar company near New York City. Nowadays you'll find him speaking at conferences, looking for the next great place to scuba dive, and sipping a glass of single malt—all while teaching everything he knows about branding, entrepreneurship, and life through his top-ranked (and rated) podcast, *The Brand You Podcast*.

Social:

- » Website: https://mikekim.com
- » Instagram: https://www.instagram.com/mikekimtv
- » Facebook: https://www.facebook.com/mikekimtv
- » Twitter: https://twitter.com/mikekimtv
- » LinkedIn: https://www.linkedin.com/in/mikekimtv/
- » YouTube: https://www.youtube.com/c/MikeKim

Possible Episode Headlines:

1. The 8 Steps to Building a Profitable Personal Brand Business

2. How to Write Persuasive Copy in a Voice That Is Unmistakably Yours

Suggested Interview Questions:

1. How do you help brands, businesses, or leaders find clarity as to what to say in their messaging?

Mike will share about his Personal Brand 3 framework, just 3 simple questions he uses to help people get clarity. Key takeaway: Marketing isn't about closing a sale, it's about opening a relationship.

2. What should people do first when building a brand identity? Is there an order, or is it just throwing stuff up against a wall and seeing what works?

Mike will share the 3 sub-identities of every brand, and/or a year-by-year breakdown of what he did to grow his business and brand presence. Key takeaway: Success is sequential, not simultaneous.

3. There's so much noise out there and everyone really tends to sound the same. How can a personal brand really say something that's unique?

Mike will share about his CopyProof framework: just 5 of the kinds of marketing voices today, with examples.

4. What's the best way to improve copywriting? Do you have any tips on copy that creates higher conversions?

Mike will share the exercise he used to learn copywriting early on, as well as some key phrases nearly any brand can use to boost conversions.

5. What is the best way to start from zero and figure out what skills and experiences you might be able to turn into a business?

Mike will share a simple process to help pinpoint marketable skills and experiences for anyone who is just starting out.

Acknowledgments

Many people celebrate scoring the winning run, not realizing that they were put on third base by the sacrifice and encouragement of others. Far be it from me to be one of those people.

Writing this book was like reliving the years since way back in 2009 when I first felt that my life was supposed to take a different direction. Those weren't easy years, and writing about that time was much harder than I expected. That said, there is no way I could have finished this book or gotten where I am today without the people in my corner who have my back.

Ray Edwards, I will never forget the day you told me in the Davenport Hotel, "You have what it takes to make it in this business." All I've tried to do is give people the same belief you gave me. Now you're "Grandcoach" to all the people I've coached in the years since.

Jason Clement, from day one you helped me see myself in a new light with your brilliant designs. This book is just your latest masterpiece.

Chelsea Brinkley, I do not know how I would manage my business without you. Thank you for freeing up my life so I could focus on this book. What I did to deserve a COO like you, I will never know.

Jeff Goins, you told me I was a writer, and you were the first person I actually believed. Thanks for your invaluable ideas and wit. I love our friendship.

Lauren V. Davis, thank you for the endless encouragement, innumerable texts talking me off the cliff, and for reading every chapter as I wrote this book.

Having a publisher who actually "gets" entrepreneurs is a rarity, and I am grateful for the team at Morgan James Publishing.

My world-class book coach, Karen Anderson (StrategicBook-Coach.com), whom I am also privileged to call a friend. Your guidance, wisdom, and brilliance are all over this book, and it would simply not exist without you.

My business coach, Todd Herman, thanks for challenging me to show up as a leader, step into my alter ego, and close the gaps between where I am and where I'm going.

My spiritual guide, Loren Trlin, you have helped me open my soul, get clarity on what I want in life, and helped me pull my future into the present.

To my family in Washington, DC, who has seen the behind-the-curtain "blood, sweat, and tears" that it's taken to write this book. My sister, Esther, brother-in-law, Sawyer, and my two nephews, Haru and Taeho, your door and refrigerator were always open for me to let loose. Charles, you were always there with an encouraging word and a good strong drink when I needed it.

Mom, you're the only person who has ever really understood my strange creative ways, and I think it's because you're the same way. I'm grateful I inherited your artistic traits. Thanks for providing a place for me to write. I love you.

Rami and Simba, you are the best dogs I could ever have; you were by my side for the weeks, months, and years this book represents. I miss you incredibly.

My clients and students, it is you whom I proudly serve. Your trust is sacred, your courage is inspiring, and I'm honored to have played a small part in your journey.

Finally, Psalm 109:27.

About the Author

Mike Kim believes marketing isn't about closing a sale, it's about opening a relationship. This refreshing approach has made him a sought-after speaker, online educator, copywriter, and consultant to some of today's top thought leaders and personal brands. Nowadays you'll find him speaking at conferences, looking for the next great place to scuba dive, and occasionally sipping a glass of single malt—all while coaching, serving clients, and recording his top-ranked (and rated) podcast, the *Brand You Podcast*.

Subscribe and Listen to The Brand You Podcast with Mike Kim

Consistently ranked as a top-ranked and 5-star rated show in personal branding, The Brand You Podcast is designed to help you showcase your unique expertise and build a highly profitable, personally fulfilling business.

A mix of solo shows and insightful interviews, each episode draws from my experience as a brand strategist, business coach, and copywriter for some of today's most influential coaches, speakers, and creators.

FIND THE SHOW ON ALL MAJOR PODCAST OUTLETS OR GO TO:

mikekim.com/show

Launch Your Business with the *You Are the Brand* Online Course.

A Step-By-Step Online Course To Help You Validate Your Audience, Offer, Pricing, and Business Model

- ✓ My proven 3-step formula for creating messages that sell
- ✓ Step-by-step "Director's Cuts" of me guiding you through my highest grossing sales and marketing campaigns
- ✓ Your very own copies of my exact brand-building scripts (used to gross over $1M in sales)
- ✓ Expert interviews with 6 and 7-figure personal brands
- ✓ Complete behind-the-scenes walkthrough of a successful personal brand campaign

FIND OUT MORE:

youarethebrandcourse.com

A free ebook edition is available with the purchase of this book.

To claim your free ebook edition:

1. Visit MorganJamesBOGO.com
2. Sign your name CLEARLY in the space
3. Complete the form and submit a photo of the entire copyright page
4. You or your friend can download the ebook to your preferred device

Morgan James
BOGO™

A **FREE** ebook edition is available for you or a friend with the purchase of this print book.

CLEARLY SIGN YOUR NAME ABOVE

Instructions to claim your free ebook edition:
1. Visit MorganJamesBOGO.com
2. Sign your name CLEARLY in the space above
3. Complete the form and submit a photo of this entire page
4. You or your friend can download the ebook to your preferred device

Print & Digital Together Forever.

Snap a photo

Free ebook

Read anywhere

www.ingramcontent.com/pod-product-compliance
Lightning Source LLC
Jackson TN
JSHW080159141224
75386JS00029B/938